A BRIGHT TOUCH OF LIFE

UNCONVENTIONAL WISDOM FOR HAPPY LIVING

BY TALIA SHEFI

Published By: DNP Presents an Imprint of Veritas Publishing House

Library of Congress Cataloging-in-Publication Data has been applied for

ISBN: 979-8-9957286-5-8

PRINTED IN THE UNITED STATES OF AMERICA

We are all connected like train tracks.

We are all moving on the train of life,

to the same destination.

Talia Shefi

Dedicated to my mom, Alisha.

ACKNOWLEDGEMENTS

To Louisa Cox. I'm enormously grateful to you, my dearest friend, my supporter, my editor, for all the help that you have given me. Without you, this book could not have been born. You have been like the metronome on my writing piano. Your devotion, your presence, and your belief in me have made it happen. Also, your wisdom, sweetness, and your honesty. You gave me the best advice when you said, *"Talia, don't talk too much about God.... just bring Him up."* I have been fortunate to have you.

Additional thanks must go to:

John Kooperberg, my second editor, for your presence in my life to help with this mission. Thank you for your hours, your kindness, and your ability to work with me. You remind me again that the right people come at the right time. Thank you for being such a wonderful, beautiful person.

Rabbi Mendy Goldstein. Thank you for listening, helping, and arranging for my contact with John.

To my dearest friend and transcriber, Pamela Anne McIntosh, who lives just next door. My hero in my life. I really appreciate your wonderful editing, support, and your golden heart.

To dear Heidi Brockbank out there in the U.S.A. My professional editing adviser ~ I thank you from the bottom of my heart for your lovely words and amazing editing. You have been like a bird that sits on my shoulders and whispers lyrics to my music. I'm blessed to know you.

Troy Lissette, for your love and for all the hours that you have patiently listened to me talk about this book. I am grateful to have you in my life.

Also, my gratitude to my sweet parents, my best friends. Thank you for being such a wonderful encouragement to me.

I am grateful to all my dear friends and to all the people that I have been associated with. Thank you for letting me play *"Life"* with you. The game is not over…let me thank the players that I still have to meet. I am excited to play *"Life"* with you all.

To my sister friend Samantha Jayne Miller – Thank you for introducing me to Trunnis Goggins II. Your friendship, love, and unwavering support mean more to me than words can express. I am deeply grateful to walk this journey with you.

To Trunnis Goggins II, from the bottom of my heart, thank you for allowing this book to come alive. Your belief in me and in this book gave it wings. I truly do not have enough words to express my gratitude. Thank you, my friend.

To DNP Presents, an imprint of Veritas Publishing House – Thank you for your professionalism, dedication, and care in bringing this book into the world. I am sincerely grateful.

Thank you to Nichol Perricci from Veritas Publishing House for the amazing editing and support.

And thank you to my talented photographer friend, Nicoline Dickinson, who captured the real me.

And to you, dear reader- Thank you for picking up this book. I hope you enjoy this journey with me and that these pages touch your heart as deeply as they came from mine.

Last but not least, to my Father, my Creator, My Love, my Best Friend, my God. Thank you for giving me this life to become what I am. Thank you for the "Wake-up Alarm" and the drum that have driven me to write this book. Thank you for unconditional love, for inspiration, for letting this book be written.

TABLE OF CONTENTS

A BRIGHT TOUCH OF LIFE

UNCONVENTIONAL WISDOM FOR HAPPY LIVING

BY TALIA SHEFI

FIRST CONTACT

Shalom, my love, it's Mum here. Can you hear me? Can you see me? Can you feel how fast my heart is beating just because of this contact with you? My beautiful darling, how are you?

I was going to write this book after I married your father, my true love and soul mate, and when I was finally feeling at home. My biggest wish was to write this book for you, my darling, my love, my only one; my daughter who exists, unborn, on the other side of life. I wanted to write to you when I was pregnant and expecting you. I haven't managed all of that yet, but even so, I feel pushed to write to you now. There's a drumming in my head. The feeling is so strong I cannot ignore it. It's clear for me, like crystal, that it is the right time to contact you. I've dropped everything else so that I can complete this book. I'm totally devoted to you.

No matter what reality shows me, I have to write to you.

Wherever you are, my sweet soul, flying between worlds, I know you can feel me. I'm here for you, waiting for you, always. I don't know why I need to write to you. Maybe it's because I need to convince you to come to this world. Whatever the reason, I know there is a connection between us. I have so many things to share with you, so many things to tell you. I love you, and I want you to know that.

Darling, there has been fun in my life, but to welcome you to this earth would be the biggest adventure of my life, the very top of the mountains. However long it takes until we meet, I will never give up on the moment, the moment when we meet.

MY PROMISE TO YOU

My darling, my sweet love, this story I'm going to tell you is my story. But I hope it will become part of your story as well. From the moment you take your first breath, and I hold you in my arms, our stories will be entwined. To understand your own story as it unfolds, you need some backstory. So I will show you the way I experience life. This story shares my point of view, the way I came to be how I am. It doesn't mean your life is going to be the same, not at all. You will write your own pages in the story of your life. But you are also part of my story. So I'm going to tell you about the love and the light to be found in life, but also about the darkness in the heart and the darkness in the soul. I'm going to tell you about people I've met, and I'm going to be very honest with you. I can't be anything else with you, for you already know me. I hope I will not scare you or make you change your mind about coming here. From now on, I'm going to connect with you forever.

THE BEGINNING OF THE BEGINNING

My darling, before you choose to enter mortality, I have to tell you something very important. This life is not real. It's really an illusion. It's like a big play. This world is like the backyard of God. So hurry up! Please don't take the decision to come here so seriously.

Life is holy. I believe that. I don't know where this belief came from, but I do believe that this world is the place that gives you the opportunity to break free from old patterns and from negativity about yourself. We do this by choosing. Life is a mixture of light and dark, and this life is the stage where you can become who you really are.

Life gives you opportunity to experience this unique element of this world. By living here, we learn about life. We learn from our feelings and thoughts. We learn what it feels like to be hungry, or to be happy, or sad. We learn through our body how to feel cold or warm. How it feels to walk, how it feels to talk through our mouth. How it feels to be part of the group – or to be rejected. We learn to feel water and fire. How it feels to be tired or alert. From the moment we arrive here, we are bombarded with so many new experiences.

All of us, from the beginning of our life here on earth until we pass through the veil at the end of our journey, are in the most exciting school in the universe. And to be able to study and experience the lessons life has to offer, our pure soul dons a physical body, through which we can learn through thought and feeling. Our experiences, both bitter and sweet, are our teachers. Our life's play starts, and an illusion settles over our mind; we forget the other world that we came from. We start to feel that who we are is our own body, thoughts, and feelings. Every human on earth HAS something very special, very extraordinary, very beautiful, very holy, very terrific, very magnificent – an ability to experience the world.

The sweetest of sweetness, the purest of pure, the brightest of bright, delight from light, biggest from the biggest, unlimited from unlimited, this is what we call our soul.

We are all souls that come into the world to play life together. The illusion of life sometimes blinds us to our true nature. Our physical eyes see only warts and wrinkles, scars and cellulite. We forget that under the illusion, we are indescribably beautiful and brilliant than we can ever realise. We are an explosion of light from a place that is all light. We come into this world to magnify that light and share it with all who cross our path.

We are all blessed and loved unconditionally by God, and we are all brothers and sisters – a cosmic family. We are all like a puzzle – every part is important to create the big picture: nobody is less, nobody is more. If some part of the puzzle is missed, the picture is not perfect. Some parts are close to each other, some parts are far away, but we are all connected, always. And we come in from The One; from God. Our mortal bodies are separate, but our spiritual souls are forever connected with each other and with our Creator.

After a long time in the world, we can forget this. Our souls start to distance themselves from light and love, and we start to believe the illusions that say we are less than wonderful.

Please, my darling, don't feel bad about your faults. You are not the only one who has them. All of us here are full of them. My darling, I know you are supposed to come here, so you probably have work to do. I have lots of work to do, too. I know that because I am still alive.

When we start to believe about our faults, our self-criticizing voice in our head whispers to us that we are not good enough. That we are flawed. That we don't deserve to be loved. That nobody cares about us. That we are not important.

When that happens, it means we've fooled ourselves into thinking our illusion is reality; we forget who we are. We cover our light with fear, our self-acceptance with self-hatred. It happens to everyone – some of us less, some of us more. We all need to overcome some negative doubt about ourselves.

My darling, my love, my only one, life is an adventure to figure out who you really are, and I know sometimes it can be hard.

But I will try to help you here. I'm going to give you a name that expresses who you really are. If during your life you forget, remember your name. It represents your true essence.

Are you ready for your name?

It's coming now.

Your name is *'Explosion of Love.'*

Where are you?

Who are you, my darling?

What is the reason you need to come here? Are you going to be the *"Bird's Glance"*? Like the birds that sing and spread love everywhere they go, your presence in life will be to spread love.

Or are you going to depress every second person you meet? Maybe you are going to be the one who fights for the Truth? Or perhaps be the person who gives others a chance to become better? Or maybe you will come here to teach me about limits and discipline. In this case, maybe don't come. No, no, no, I'm joking! Whatever the reason is for you to come here, my arms are open to you. I'm here, waiting for you.

YOUR BIGGEST CRISIS

My darling, my sweet, sweet soul, there is no other way to come here but to be born. I wish I could make it easier for you and just give you my address. Then you could fall from the sky in a soft bassinet and just knock on my door. But it doesn't work like that. Unfortunately, storks don't fly in the air with babies. All of us get here by being born. That's just how it is. The nice part is that before we are born, we are created by making love, by a push of energy that slides us into the world. When we die, it is different, but as sad as death is from a mortal perspective, it is still the beginning of a new life and a new journey. We all arrive through the front door of love, and when our time is over, we pass away through a different door. Nobody knows how or what happens next, but I believe we return to the realm of love and light that we existed in before coming to this world.

I think to be born is the biggest crisis you will ever have to go through, darling. The moment you come out, you will cry and scream. Actually, until you do, everyone in the room with us will wait with bated breath until they hear you cry. Your first breath is going to be really hard and scary, I know, but you will have the breath of this life with you until you die.

When you arrive, you will be in the world of illusion. Your spirit will be locked in your body, your *"fake"* new home. You will feel emotions for the first time, wonder and laughter, but also sorrow and anger. In Judaism, we say that the groove between your nose and lips is the mark left by the touch of an angel that has made you forget the other world.

The moment you arrive, and you are screaming and crying, maybe because you start to feel life, and you feel a twinge of homesickness for the world you just left, I will be there for you. I will take you immediately and hold you in my arms. I will kiss you softly. I will put you close to my heart. You will hear the beating of my heart. I will tell you again and again, *"I love you, my darling. Welcome to the world. I'm your Mum."*

YOUR CHOOSING

Darling, my sweet love, look at me very carefully. I want you to know that you are the one who has chosen me, and there is a reason for that. The day may come when you complain about me. Perhaps I've told you no -- you can't eat your candy before dinner, or you have to do your chores before you play, or you can't go to the concert because you haven't done your homework. Maybe I will march you back to the store to apologize for stealing the ice-cream bar.

So please, if you ever complain about me, remember that you chose me. You know, I have this feeling when I think about you. I am positive that you are full of love and joy. Full of energy and creativity. I can almost see you. Can you see me? Our souls recognize each other, even though in this life we've yet to meet. So when we look into each other's eyes for the first time, I make you a promise: I will always try to be truly who I am with you, because of my love for you. You can trust me.

This means that I will always, always be true to myself and honest with you. By doing this and by checking that I'm always listening to my heart, I will give you the best of me. All the things that will come out in our journey together will be guided by the strongest power in the world--the power of love.

Now I have to let you in on a little secret: real love sometimes comes disguised. But you can learn to recognize it, because it is always concerned with what's best for others. It always wants the beloved to find true joy. It always seeks to help people become their truest self.

For example, if someone's child has lied and his mother punished him for this, it's an act of love. Because, although she is tough with him, she is guided by love and gives him the opportunity to check his behavior and make a better choice. She is helping him back to his heart.

I will check myself always, no matter what. I will always act from a place of love. Because when we love someone unconditionally, as I already love you, we always look inside ourselves. We open up our hearts and souls to the universe to figure out what is the right way to help our beloved. What is the best way for us to be? Because love is unlimited. We open our heart, and by doing so, we can open more windows in our heart, and allow love to grow in us like sun on a blossom.

When love fills our heart, it teaches us the real meaning of life. What an amazing feeling; we will do anything for someone we love. And I will do everything for you, my darling. When you love someone, you can truly change the world. Nothing seems impossible. For you, I could climb to the sky and grab a star. No challenge seems too daunting.

For you, I would face my deepest fear. No sacrifice is too great. Filled with love, we find it is sweet to live, love, serve, change, and yes, even die for our loved ones. And that's the challenge and the gift that our loved ones give us: they help us act from a place of love.

And from the place of love and in the name of the power of love, I promise to you I will be in my heart as much as I can.

For me, the beginning of life was hard. I actually struggled for many years with the question of whether to live or not to live. Despite the love and support of my parents, I remember feeling as if there was a big hole in my life. I felt unwanted, unloved. I felt forgotten and lost. I felt as if I was very old but with a young body. I thought many times about suicide. I don't know where this feeling came from. I believe that when I arrived on earth, I already carried with me this idea from the other world.

I believe that one of the many things I came here to overcome was the untrue idea that I was not supported by God. I believed that I was meant to live this life unsupported, that everything was in my own hands, to manage on my own. This false idea is based on my faults and my weaknesses, on some hurt that I carry inside my soul, for I'm not sure how long. But I know that the reason that I live on earth is to learn that this belief is false, and for life to heal me, and to show me the truth--that I am supported and loved by God a hundred percent.

When I was seven, I remember a very intense moment in my life, I said to myself: *"I will either commit suicide now, or I will never, ever think about committing suicide ever again."*

Until that time, I had thought about committing suicide a lot, but nobody knew what was happening inside myself to come to this point. I didn't show anybody the struggle that was happening inside my mind, inside my soul.

Two thoughts helped push me to the light, to choose life. One of them was that if I committed suicide, I would hurt my family forever. They would blame themselves for my action--which did not connect with them at all. Suicide is a personal decision. Nobody in the world can compel someone to choose life or to not choose life. I've met people who have taken on so much guilt from their loved one committing suicide; I've wanted to jump out of my skin and let them know that they couldn't save someone who didn't choose life.

Committing suicide is an intimate, personal decision that is made from within. Nobody can stop someone's decision to end their life – not even by being there for them twenty-four hours a day. Not even by offering unlimited support. It's all about that one person; nobody knows the thoughts in someone else's mind or how they perceive their own life. Only they can choose to live. You can't choose that for them.

So the guilt and the *what ifs* should not exist. Because you can't stop anybody from making this decision. It is not connected to anybody else. It is about the inner life that only that person deals with. To choose life is a personal commitment. To choose death is the same. It's also a decision that we need to respect.

The second thought that came to me, and pushed me to not commit suicide, was the thought that if I'm alive, there has to some purpose to life, (maybe I was here to feed the neighbour's cat? As a child, that seemed like a serious contender for my life's mission,) and while I may not see that now, I would give myself the time to figure it out. (The cat will come to me.) At that moment, I promised myself I would experience this life to figure it out.

It was such a strong moment for me because after I decided to live, I never thought about suicide again.

Here is the truth that I learned from that moment: when you make a decision, you become stronger, and when you make a decision that is right for you, life will reward you.

At another point in my life, I made another life-changing decision that I will never forget. I was about seventeen, and I had been crying all night long in bed because I felt so lost, so far away from myself. I felt far away from who I was. As I lay there in the darkness, I yearned to believe that something bigger than me, bigger than everything, exists and that something (which I call God) wants me close to him. Something whispered in my heart that he was waiting for me to choose him, to find a way to open up some road inside myself that would make me feel a connection. A connection to love. I decided at that moment to turn to God.

I said over and over again, "Please help me!" Well, something started happening. Inside me, each day, I could feel something changing. I felt as if a guardian arrived, reached down and held my hand, so that for the first time I wasn't alone. I felt cared for, protected, and loved, and I also felt a love for myself, growing. Instead of focusing my attention on other people's lives, and constantly wondering how it was they seemed to know what to do, I started to consider my own life, with hope and optimism for the future. I stopped thinking that I was stupid and that I had nothing to offer the world, and that the world had nothing for me.

The funny thing is that as a result of the changes in me, I started to get more love and attention from other people, which surprised me. I learned that the key to accepting who I am is simply to love myself. The key to loving other people is to love them without need. The world is a reflection of what is happening inside you.

When I started to love myself, and began to think positively about myself, by myself, without anybody saying to me anything, just my mind to myself, I started to notice that people reacted to me in the same way--with warmth, acceptance, and optimism. When I didn't love myself, people reacted to the disbelief inside of me by ignoring me. But once I loved myself, people supported this belief by giving me more attention.

It was like whatever thoughts I addressed myself became what I saw in the mirror.

I have to tell you this, my darling, just so you know where I came from and what was my biggest challenge in life. I believe that we choose our parents before we arrive in this world. And I believe that one of the biggest questions that everyone should ask themselves is 'why are you my parent?' and then take full responsibility that we have chosen them. It may take a lifetime to fully understand, but trust that you have made the right decision in selecting them even before you were born. Your parents are the most qualified people in the universe to help you to become who you were meant to be.

My parents were perfect for me because they gave me the space I needed; I needed time to explore and expand my knowledge. I needed freedom to figure out life and to find myself. To allow me this space was an act of love. But that's for me, and that's who I am. Everyone is different.

Now, my darling. What do you need from me?

I'm so thrilled you've chosen me, my darling. The journey that we walk together will help both of us to grow. I will give you a strong foundation, from which you can grow. I will provide shelter for your body and your soul. I will nourish your heart and your mind. I will dream a life of joy and wonder for you and do my best to help you find and reach your own dreams in your own perfect way. And you will fill me with laughter, and so I will find hope everywhere. And you will sometimes also fill me with tears, and so I will grow in empathy for others. I couldn't ask for a better travelling companion. And you can always lean on me, no matter where our path leads us.

You will challenge me to be better, and I will always act towards you from a place of love.

The meeting between both of us is so strong because we have something in our souls that attracted us to be together. As mother and daughter.

I can't wait to experience this meeting with you, that destiny that comes from the higher realm.

Your choosing.

Soul to soul.

Human to human.

I'm here, my darling, waiting to be chosen by you.

ABOUT BELIEF

My daring, my love, my only one. Life is amazing, and one of the reasons it is so is that Earth holds so many expressions of God. Life on this dazzling jewel of a world is a smorgasbord designed to enchant. Every corner of the world is filled with infinite variety, in any category you can name. Snow-capped mountains, verdant jungles, and breathtaking desert vistas. Flowers in every shade. Trees from baobab to sequoia to willow. Mighty rivers like the Amazon or small meadow brooks. Animals, wild and tame. Whale and minnow. Ancient empires and modern cities, rustic country villages, and practical everyday suburbs. So many cultures and countries--each with gifts for the mind, body, and soul. Food and music, art and literature, sports and entertainment. Religion and philosophy. So many smells. So many languages. So many of so many things.

If we had in this world just one view of food, culture, or color, how would we learn about differences? How could we choose between accepting differences or rejecting differences? We have to have something that offers contrast in our life, and something that represents the opposite of us. Then we will get the chance to choose – to embrace or reject. It's in that ability to choose between things, both opposites as well as things similar in nature, that we learn what we value and love. In exercising this gift, we also learn to see with better eyes, to see beyond the surface.

We can choose to see the beauty that is present in every person, or we can decide that what is different.

We look different on the outside. But still, everyone has two eyes, one nose, two ears, one heart. We look so different, but actually we look the same. It all depends on how we choose to view things.

I believe that one of the biggest challenges we have to learn about differences now (and during our entire history) is how to accept each other's religion or spiritual mood. To see the beauty and the colourful message that comes from each philosophy. But it is here that too often we fail.

Because each faith declares that they are the only one who knows how to work for God, that they are the only group that speaks for him, and that all the rest are invalid.

This belief betrays the highest good in every religion or spiritual mood, because it creates separation from our common brotherhood, our human beginnings.

We can choose to see the beauty in our different views of God, in the unique way we come to find God, instead of judging others for believing differently than we do.

We can honor our own beliefs and share them respectfully with others, without judgment of others.

A good way to do this is to ask, *"Is my belief coming from a place of love or a place of fear?"*

Let me tell you a story about belief.

One day, a new client came to see me for a massage. John was a wrinkly fifty-six-year-old man with grey hair, blue eyes, and very hairy eyebrows. He actually looked like he was in his early seventies. He had a deep voice and walked hunched over.

As I always do before a treatment with a new client, I asked John about his medical history. Apparently, he had survived two major heart attacks. Out of the blue, John asked me, *"Where are you from, Talia?"*

"I'm from Israel," I said.

"Are you Jewish?"

The forceful way he asked made me feel uncomfortable. I felt almost as if I had to apologize for being Jewish.

"Yes, I am Jewish," I said. I got from John such a disappointed look. Without warning, he launched into a lecture.

"If you want to go to heaven, Talia, you need to become Christian. The only way for you is to accept Jesus as the only Son of God. I am giving you a chance to save yourself. It's not too late for you." John's voice got louder and louder, and now he

started pointing at me with his finger. *"You have to do it! Jesus says that he is the only son from God."* John was practically screaming by now, his expression serious and intense. *"If you don't do it, Talia, you will burn in hell. I am giving you the chance to save yourself."* Now his intensity was so extreme, I thought he was going to have an orgasm. Or maybe another heart attack.

I was shocked. I didn't know whether to laugh or cry as John asked, *"So what do you say, Talia? Are you going to save your soul?"*

"Are you finished with your speech, John?" I asked. *"Would you like a glass of water? You are overexcited and breathing very fast. You need to relax a little bit."*

John's eyes widened.

"Now I'm going to talk and you are going to listen to me," I said. *"What is all this bullshit you are telling me now? You are the victim of fear, and you are covering it up with your religion. God doesn't have religions. The purpose of all religions is to help you be free from fear and listen to your heart. It doesn't matter what you say; it matters how you are with yourself and others. You are the son of God. I am the daughter of God. We are all His children. Do you really believe what you are saying about hell? It's just an image, a symbol. You don't need to die to be there. When you live free of fear, then you will find the state of heaven in your heart."*

I stopped talking, and there was silence. I was one hundred percent sure about what I said to him. What was I feeling at that moment? I felt quiet in my heart. I needed to trust my feelings and wait.

After a moment, John stood up in front of me. He looked into my eyes and with a soft, quiet voice, he said, *"Can I shake your hand? Thank you."*

I never saw John again. But I have sympathy in my heart for him. I know his belief is based on fear, and it's not his fault. He may have grown up in a family or community that believes in the same way; he may not have had an opportunity to hear different beliefs.

The fact that he thanked me about my belief shows that even someone with an extremely fanatic belief, based on fear, can change his mind. Because a belief based on love can overcome every fear.

The way to do that is by free, sincere, open communication. If we meet someone whose beliefs are based on fear, instead of fighting or pushing him away, we can always show a different belief – a belief based on love.

And also love comes through us when we bring love to those that can't bring it to themselves. Everyone can believe whatever they want to, but our belief affects our thinking, our actions, our emotion, our health. And beliefs that teach and preach against a particular group of people – perhaps

Muslim, Jewish, Christian, gay – is belief that teaches us hate and is controlled by fear. Some people may use this fear to control and manipulate others.

Belief born out of love teaches us to accept each other as an expression of God.

I want you, my darling, to ask yourself: *"From which place is my belief based?"*

The answer has to be love.

PEOPLE CAN CHANGE YOUR LIFE

My sweet soul, my darling, when you arrive in this world, you will sleep a lot at first. Then, slowly, you will begin to feel more and more comfortable. When you are ready, I will introduce you to so many amazing, wonderful people. I am blessed to have true friends with big hearts, and I know you will love them. For me, true happiness is friendship--to be surrounded by loving people and to return that love.

My darling, you are going to meet so many people in your life, too. Not all of us meet the same types of people, though. What is it that attracts people to us in our life? Is it our beliefs or destiny? Whatever it is, I know you are going to meet people who will light up your heart. People can change your life just by the way they live, by the way they express themselves, and by the way they make you feel. What an amazing feeling to connect with people who accept one another without judgment. To have loving friends is to be rich.

At the same time, my darling, it's important to remember that there are many other people who come here with different stories. Assume you are going to be the Bird's

Glance – as in, everywhere you will go, people will experience love and happiness, just like constant birdsong.

And then, for example, you meet someone who comes here to, let's say, learn to be more loving. So, in the beginning of his journey, he will only be concerned about himself and will be very selfish. The meeting between both of you could then be very painful for you, because he only thinks of himself and will drag your energy down.

There are people who cheat on themselves. They wear jackets of fear, boots of weakness, and rings of lies. That's their choice. If life introduces you to these kinds of people, just remind yourself that it's not your responsibility to change them. The only thing you need to change is the way you feel about them. Because remember, my darling, we never know what's going on in someone else's life. People react from their reality, from their situation. Not always because of you.

After all, maybe the grumpy person in the line at the store is hurt and is in terrible pain; maybe the person who gives you the cold shoulder at the office is an only child and grew up super-shy; maybe your friend from work ignored you all day because she forgot to wax her moustache and she's self-conscious about it. Maybe your neighbour that shouted at you in the evening because earlier that day she caught her husband sleeping with someone else, on her new bed, on her new sheets – that came all the way from Venice!

Maybe the person who never has any sympathy for anyone around them has never had the blessing of being sick, or ill, or broke (and therefore has never had the accompanying blessing of learning empathy and compassion).

We can't take responsibility for other people's actions or words, but we can take responsibility to how we respond.

All of us are sometimes disappointed by other people. So what? Put more attention on positive people.

Ask yourself, my darling, *"What makes me feel good? To run? To read? To cook?"* Ask yourself, *"Who are the people in my life that when I speak with them or hang out with them, I feel unconditional love?"* Go with the love, the light, as often as you can.

When someone touches your heart, it is a gift because it means we have a chance to change our views. Sometimes this experience can affect our whole life.

Let me tell you a story, my darling, about a trip that changed my life.

I was twenty-seven years old and living in Israel. (Don't ask me how long ago that is!) I felt stuck and bored in life. I didn't know what to change or what to do to feel more engaged in life. Around the same time, one of my friends, Alina (one day you will meet her), asked me to visit her. She's Israeli like me, but she had been living for five years in Paris. It always made me happy to meet her. She was always so bubbly, full of life and enthusiasm, and she was always doing something interesting.

She told me about all the fun she was having in Paris and promised that we were going to have heaps of fun if I came to visit.

What I really admire about Alina is her honesty. She told me of the difficulties she had experienced when she first arrived in Paris and decided to stay there, but now her life was just fun, fun, fun. When I met with Alina and saw how much she enjoyed her life, it made me want to feel the same way. There was something so vibrant about her. I thought about her often, how cool she is. But how could I go to Paris? I had a job. I couldn't take time off. I rented a house, and I had no savings. I thought it was impossible.

A few days after Alina asked me to go to Paris, I met with my dear friend, Ayal. You will meet him one day, too. His heart is the size of the Atlantic Ocean. He is the best listener ever. I told him about how Alina inspired me.

Ayal said, *"Why don't you go?"*

"How can I go, Ayal? I've never travelled by myself before, and I don't have the money."

"Let's talk it through," he said. Slowly, slowly, during our conversation, I started to think that I could actually do it. I realised that visiting Paris was not just a dream or a fantasy. A few days after my conversation with Ayal,

I decided, *"That's it. I'm going!"*

Sometimes it takes me such a long time to make a decision. Sometimes it takes weeks or months, but once I make a decision, I have to do it IMMEDIATELY. Now! I can't do anything else. I can't wait. Otherwise, I will die. That's something about me, my darling, that I've tried to change many times, but I can't.

I can't remember now how I found the money for the trip, but guess what, my darling? Within the very same week, I was on a plane to Paris. Sitting on the plane, headed to Paris, my fantasies sped up, faster than the speed of light. Aha! So this is why I haven't settled down yet. Because all this time I needed to live in Paris! Maybe I will meet the man of my dreams there, and then we'll move to the Caribbean. How cool would that be? Or maybe we'll move to New York! Maybe a talent scout will discover me on the banks of the Seine and turn me into a famous Hollywood actor. I couldn't wait! *"À tout alors! Paris, I'm coming!!"*

When I landed in Paris, I expected to see Alina in the arrivals area, but she wasn't there. I called her. *"Welcome to Africa!"* she said when she answered the phone. *"Haha, no,*

Paris. Welcome to Paris! Talia, you will have to take a taxi because I'm still at work in the bar."

"Yes, sure, all good," I said. But I was thinking, Holy shit, how do I get a taxi here?

With Alina's help, and after she had talked to a taxi driver and given him the address and directions, I arrived at the bar. Alina had been working there for a few years. It was such a cool place. I felt like I was in the theatre.

"Hello, darling!" Alina said, giving me a big smile and a big hug. "Everyone, meet Talia," she said. Salut! Hello!

"Want something to drink?" someone asked.

"Don't ask her – just bring the glass!" said Alina.

I sat at the bar. The bar was full and loud. Alina ran from table to table and talked with everyone. All the people reacted so positively to her, laughing and joking. She was the heart of the place. Alina made drinks so fast, rushing to tables, and all the time she was laughing. Watching her work made me happy. She was living in the moment. After a few hours, the place became quieter, and she came over to me.

"Darling, we're going soon. Are you good?"

"Yes, oh yes," I said.

Alina said in Hebrew, *"Great. Everyone can fuck themselves. You're probably tired, let's go home."*

Of course, Alina had the coolest motorbike ever. We drove through Paris on the bike. The air was beating against my face, and I was so happy. I felt the promise of Paris in my heart!

We arrived at Alina's flat. Alina said to me, *"This is the coolest part of Paris."*

She was right. It was the coolest house in the coolest neighborhood, for the coolest girl. The apartment was so arty, so stylish. Day after day, we travelled around Paris on her bike. We went out at night, too. Everywhere we went, Alina talked with everyone. She sang at the bar, sometimes standing on the tables. One day, she wore swimming goggles and old-fashioned red heels, just because she felt like it. After three or four days of travelling around together like this, Alina told me she needed to get back to work and that I should continue to travel on my own. She explained how to use the metro. Yeah, right! I thought. I couldn't speak French, and my English was so basic, a three-year-old wouldn't understand me. But Alina insisted.

She gave me the timetable, told me to go wherever I wanted, and then meet her after work. *"You are part of Paris, now,"* she said.

So I did it. I followed the timetable. Of course, I didn't understand anything I read. But I looked carefully at all of the letters and matched the ones on the timetable with the signs around me. That way, I could work out where I was. I stopped people all the time and said, *"Excuse me, excuse me... I need to go here."* I would point at the map and then at a point somewhere down the street. *"Is it there?"* Sometimes, by accident, I even asked the same person twice. *"You asked me a second ago!"* they said, annoyed.

Alina was proud of me. She said, *"Talia, you are so good with the Metro! You never get lost!"*

In the evenings when I travelled around Paris, life was so good. One night in a café, I met a girl named Jaqueline, from Paris. We spoke English at the same level, which made our conversation like a chat between two deaf people who didn't know sign language. I understood from her that she was going to a party and that I was invited. I was in the mood to go with the flow, so I decided to go. We got in her car and drove to an apartment. Everyone in the apartment was sleeping, but Jaqueline woke them up. After a few minutes, the girls were dressed up, and we hopped in the car again and continued to drive to God knows where. We stopped at more than three or four houses, and each time it was the same. Everyone inside was sleeping until we arrived, and we waited for them to get dressed, and then off we went again. One of the guys in the car I was in, who spoke a bit of English, said, *"Hey, Talia, Jacqueline told me you are lost. How did that happen?"*

"I'm not lost," I said. *"I'm going to the party."*

"Oh," he said. *"You aren't lost! You think you are coming to the party?"* He started to laugh.

"What, we're not going to a party? Where are we going?"

"No, no, we are. We're going to a party now." We arrived at a house just outside of Paris, one of the flashiest houses I had ever seen. Everyone was sitting together in the living room. I made small talk with a few people, and then I went to the loo. When I got back, I didn't understand what I was seeing. On the main table, there was a mountain of white powder, and next to that, there was a mountain of diamonds. Oh... my...God. Is that heroin? Or is it cocaine? Oh shit, am I hanging out with gangsters from Paris? How do these ridiculous things keep happening to me? Oops. I may have taken this adventure too far.

Someone asked me, *"You want some? Help yourself."*

"No, no. Thank you. Merci."

All of a sudden, couples in the room started touching each other, and then other people started joining in and touching them too.

Oops. What am I doing here? The main question is: how do I get myself out?

Someone said, *"We really like you, Talia. We think you are cute."*

Oh my God. My phone started ringing. Thank God, it was Alina. *"Hi Hun,"* she said. *"Where are you?"*

"I'm at a friend's party."

"Cool!" she said. *"You make friends so fast! We're going out. Come to the bar and bring your friends with you."*

"No, no, no, that's okay. Um… they're too busy, and I don't think they're in the mood. I'm coming by myself, okay?" I decided to take a taxi to the metro, where I would match up the letters on the timetable and the signs, and ride the metro to Alina's.

"Hey, hey, guys!" I said to my new friends. *"Emergency! I have to go! I need a taxi, my friend is very sick, and I have to help her. Quick! Call a taxi!"*

Two minutes later, I was in the taxi. Fifteen minutes later, I was on the metro. Half an hour later, I was with Alina. What a relief.

That night, Alina, a few friends, and I went from club to club, dancing and drinking. Everything was so funny, so light, so wonderful. But my trip to Paris was almost over. I started to feel sad.

Before I left, I said, *"I had an amazing time with you, Alina. I don't want to go back to Israel to my boring life."*

"I don't want you to leave. Stay!" she said.

"But I can't stay, there is no way. I hold an Israeli passport, and I can't get a work visa anywhere, so I have to go back." We hugged. *"I will see you again."*

On the airplane back to Israel, I had already made another decision. I decided I would leave Israel and try my life in a different country. Even if my passport made it impossible, even if I couldn't get a work visa anywhere, I would find a way.

I felt so strongly that my experience with Alina was my calling. It left me with such a strong feeling to look inside myself and to figure out what it would mean to me to do what Alina does – to draw myself to a different reality, a different culture. To challenge myself.

Alina moved a feeling inside myself, and by seeing her, she opened my eyes. My time with her was providential. It opened my mind to new possibilities and led me to the next chapter in my life.

The role Alina played in my life was a gift from the universe. Life knew what I needed was to be *"pushed out of the nest,"* and it placed my friend at the right times and places in my life for her to inspire me.

My darling, within three months, I was on a plane to Australia, and a few years after that, I emigrated to New Zealand.

The universe communicates with us all the time. It gently maneuvers people until their paths intersect and intertwine with ours. Those are people who light up love in our heart, who take up our intention, who touch our soul, who make us look inside and question ourselves. Most likely, they are the angels in our life.

The universe puts us together to guide us to our destiny. And by the way, don't look for them. They will come to you – at the right time. You may not recognize them at first, for often they come in disguise. But you will always know them as you look back at your life's journey and see how they have helped you grow, how they have helped you reach your dreams.

So these special people are part of the equation that can help us fulfil our destiny. But there's also another part of the equation, and you are in charge of that. Let me explain. How often do we feel free to make choices and to make changes? Not that often. Not really. Our fear blocks the belief that we can choose and change. The biggest change comes first of all from letting our fear go. Then comes action.

Close your eyes and imagine what you aspire to be. What fears stand between yourself now and that vision of yourself? What holds you back from doing what you really want to do?

There are things that you really want to do that match your true nature, but you don't dare to do them because fear is holding you back. There is a song in your soul that wants to be played. This song will play in your mind over and over again until you open the door and free it with the key of courage. That key is somewhere inside you. Find it. Don't let the mountains of fear bury it. You need to dig deep, never tiring to find this key. That is the way to get from the prison of fear to the freedom of choice in life.

You have the power to make this choice, but I will warn you: one person will dare to make a choice or make a change, and ten people will stand in front of him like a wall to tell him he can't make it. When that happens, I want you to remember what I say now: Who cares what other people think about you? It's your opinion that counts here. You are the leader of your life. Nobody can take it from you.

The biggest incentive for change is the feeling of being stuck. Oh what a feeling!! You think I'm joking? Hold on, my dear darling, my sweetheart, because this feeling is actually a gift. The stronger the feeling is, the bigger the changes you will make. Open your eyes, open your heart. The answer will come through the right people and your power to choose and take action.

WISHES

When the night comes, and the sky becomes dark

and the stars are shining, the wind moves through the trees

and the rain falls gently on me,

I think of you.

Where are you now?

What are you experiencing?

What will it be like to hold you, hug you, to be there for you?

Take all the time you need.

I'm here, my love,

To support you with whatever you need.

My heart and soul are waiting for you,

for the right moment,

for when we meet in this world, the world of illusion.

ABOUT GOD

My sweet, sweet darling, it's time for a big question: What is God? When I was young, I truly believed that God lived on a cloud and had a big beard. Today, I believe he is a DJ who smokes weed all day. I'm kidding about that. But seriously, I have learned some things in my years on this world, and I will share them with you. I have come to understand that God is everywhere. God is in me when I choose him. For me, God is absolute love without fear. I think that it isn't important what you call Him; it's more important how you are with yourself and with others. I will give you a really good example.

My grandfather Zvi passed away many years ago. I wonder now, do you know him? Maybe you are sitting on his knee now, in the belly of the sun, and you can read my mind. He would never talk about himself, so let me tell you about him.

Your great-grandfather was the person who had the most God inside himself that I have ever met in all my life. He survived the Holocaust in Dachau, Germany, and the worst things happened to him. His wife and two of his daughters were murdered. He polished Nazi shoes, and sometimes he was given the skin of potatoes. That's how he survived.

When the war ended, all of the survivors ran from the ghetto (camp) to find food. They had been starving for three or four years by that time. My grandfather and one of his friends ran to an abandoned house to find something to eat. Inside the house, my grandfather whispered to his friend, *"Somebody is looking at me."*

"Where? Show me," his friend said.

But nobody was in the abandoned house. It was just a mirror. My grandfather hadn't recognised himself.

After the war, my grandfather threw away his kippah. A kippah is the small hat that Jewish men wear on top of their heads. It represents the belief that God is always with you, on top of your head.

"I don't believe in God. God doesn't exist," my grandfather said. Well, after he experienced the worst things that could ever happen to someone, losing his children and his wife to murder, I can understand why he said that. After you have seen the worst evil, how can you believe? Even God cried.

But it doesn't matter what he said; it matters how he was in life. He was the kindest, most wise man in the world. He used to say all the time, *"In life, you must never keep hate. We should not hate Germany. There are new Germans today. Don't forget your history, but never live in the past."*

Grandfather Zvi was a businessman. A few years after the war, he was engaged in business with Germany. Everyone loved him, not just loved him, adored him. He wasn't a talkative person, but when he spoke, everyone was quiet because they knew that they would hear pure wisdom. He used to say, *"Every problem that can be solved with money is not a problem. Your real problems are those that can't be solved with money."*

When he did business with people who stole his money, he would say, *"Money comes, money goes. I prefer to trust. Life is a circle. Sometimes you are at the top, other times you are at the bottom."*

When he made a mistake, he would say, *"You learn all your life, but you die stupid. In life, you need to try everything."*

When someone did a favour for my grandfather, and then turned around and disappointed him with the next thing he did, Grandfather Zvi used to say… *"It is like the cow that provides a full container of fresh milk and then kicks it over with her back hoof."*

When he was struggling with money, he would say, *"If you have one dollar, always say that you have two. Live like you have more, think like you have more, and then that will be your reality."*

My grandfather Zvi demonstrated through his actions what choosing God really means. It was clear in the way he treated people and in his ability to forgive. He always chose the positive, no matter what. That's what is important. Those are the actions of love. I want you to be proud of your ancestor, and you will be when you can exhibit the same wisdom in your own dealings with people. By actually acting with that love and forgiveness and acceptance of others, you will see there is a vast difference between talking about God and choosing God.

Action is your true belief, not words.

FINDING THE ONE

My darling, my love, my only one, I need your help. Can you do me a favour? I need you to help me find your father. Do you mind dropping a stick on his head from heaven? Send him the GPS coordinates to my house, because I think he got lost. If he is going to his girlfriend's house, redirect him. Tell him, *"Hey Dad, that's not my Mum! Turn around, the babe with the curly hair, that's my mum. She's been waiting for you for ages."*

In the meantime, I need to remind myself to be patient. How long do I need to be patient? If my wishes had already arrived, I'd already be writing to you about your father, and I'd tell you how wonderful he is and how long I had waited for him, and how the wait was worth it. I would tell you how I found pure love and friendship. I can't do that right now, but what I can tell you, my love, is not to lose faith that you will find the one, because I know I will, and in your time, you will. And when you find the one, you'll know. You'll know because of how at home you feel. You will feel a sweet quietness in your heart. It'll feel like you've known each other forever. You won't have a storm in your heart anymore, because love will no longer be a question but an experience.

In the beginning, being in love is intense and delicious. It will warm your heart, give you happiness and joy. The two of you will be connected and will share and express your inner lives. You will suit each other's lives perfectly, and you will want the same things. Any pain and disappointment from the past will be forgotten. You will understand for yourself what people mean when they talk about real connection and love that is *'meant to be'*.

This is the dream, but it doesn't always work like we envision. When people recognize the calm and the peaceful feeling, then they are with the right person. But it's not always that obvious. All of us are looking for our soul mate and our best friend. Sometimes we have a script of how they need to be: how they should look, what they need to do. Then, when the universe provides us with a perfect match for us, and it doesn't match our fantasy and our script, we struggle to receive the person. The gift wrapping doesn't match our belief of Mr. Right.

A friend shared her story with me. When she first met her husband, she was so disappointed. In her mind, she always pictured she would be with an academic man who listened to classical music. Instead, she met a man who listened to rock metal music, and he swore all the time.

After she got over her fantasy and started to feel what this man did for her, she said that nobody was more perfect for her than him. Another friend said to me, *"What? I've waited so long for this. For this lost man who's bald, who's hairy, and eats all the time, and other than ears, he probably looks like a chimpanzee."* Her soul mate came in a plain package, but he made her so happy with his humor and his kindness.

The common lesson from this is that once the women dropped the fantasy of their perfect man and started to focus on the feelings that grew between them and their partner, love was present. A strong and honest relationship developed. All of them remain together, are happy and satisfied, and say they are with *'the one.'*

Sometimes it's funny how we can't see that the right person is in front of us. But when true love presents itself, we cannot ignore it. As long as we give it a chance, we can hope for an amazing gift.

Now, back to reality. I'm not with your father yet, my love, but I will be. I don't doubt it, just as I know I will hold you in my arms one day. Just as I know you will find *The One.*

Maybe you will meet your true love at eighteen. Or maybe you will meet a lot of different men before you find your heart's companion. My darling, my love, everyone goes through different experiences. Who knows what you will go through? I hope you won't be like me because I've been through a lot. It feels like up till now, I've been living with an invisible note on my forehead which says, *"If you are in the middle of your biggest life drama, if you are on the cross, or suffer from some mental illness, come here! Come to me! I will give you my heart. You can use it, step on it, and then throw it away."* I can tell you that I have found my heart on the floor too many times.

My darling, I'm done playing Mother Theresa. I'm ready to find the one, your own father, and I want you, my darling. No matter how long it takes, I will not accept anything less than the right man for me.

Once, I travelled by bus all the way from Cambodia to Vietnam with a broken heart. I locked myself in the hotel for two days in Vietnam, under the water of the shower, to try to release the pain in my heart. Another time, I was working in the south of New Zealand with a broken heart; the same way, every day, with a feeling of a sword stuck in my heart. Almost waiting for someone to help me to remove the sword, because it was so painful.

Why is rejection so painful?

I will try to help you understand how face rejection with grace and strength, my darling, although I hope you will never have to experience it, ever.

The way I understand it, rejection is connected with three words: **trust, expectation, and self-esteem.**

TRUST

Trust plays a big role. Because if we hold the belief that everything that happens to us is delivered from the universe, then we need to trust that things will work out for the best, even when this guy that we love so much right now is gone. We need to trust that it's working perfectly for us. Even if we cannot see it right now. Maybe this trust can take down the volume of pain felt in the heart.

EXPECTATION

Expectation happens when we meet someone that we like. All our fantasies start to go on overdrive. First of all, we make time to open our heart, then we accept to receive the same (or more!). Then we decide that this is The One, and straight away our mind tells a story. We see our life together, married, children, and just as we're about to buy a house (in our mind) he's disappeared. And we never hear from him again.

"Why are you leaving? We just bought a house?" To this, he replies, *"What are you talking about?"*

I'm sure after I publish this book, nobody in the world will want to be with me. I'm too strange.

Expectation that doesn't happen is like two people travelling in a lift, but each of them exit on different levels.

Their lives may never meet together. The expectation will not match.

Actually, what I realised is that rejection does not really happen. Because the other way to look at it is as *'protection'*. You're never rejected; it's the universe's way of protecting you because the person isn't right for you. You will realise this in time.

SELF-ESTEEM

If we value ourselves more and love ourselves more. And we come to a point where we love ourselves no matter who else loves us, we will come to a point where we see ourselves in OUR eyes, not others' eyes, maybe we will be more cool about rejection. To be rejected by someone means nothing; it doesn't mean that we are not good enough, not good enough, not equal. It just means that this person doesn't choose us, that's all.

We back ourselves. Our love to ourselves, we are still great, good, wonderful!

But even though the pain is still there. So what can we do?

I have a recipe, medicine, that always works. But to receive it, you will have to travel with me.

Are you ready, my darling?

Come travelling with mum. I'm going to show you show you something magnificent.

Close your eyes, and stretch your hands in the air. We fly now to the sky. We go through the clouds, it's so nice up here. We're going to stretch ourselves more, coming into the sun it's so warm here, and safe.   Now, a little bit of a jump. We arrive in Space.

Woah! It's so quiet here. And the stars sparkle, twinkle, shining so bright.

Let's stay here a little bit. Our quiet time. Let's be tender, a little bit still. Melt into the moment.

Conform to the time – without time.

This is not our last destination. We are going to enter a place of all good. All thoughtful. All light.

We're going to meet the Creator.

Now, my darling, we stand in front of him, and we're going to ask a question. A very clear question, because when we want a specific answer, we need to be specific in the question.

So, we come to the place that is all good and blessed; 100 per cent light. And we met The One who loves us unconditionally; he wants only the good for us, just the light. We ask the question: *"So you're the one who loves me unconditionally and wants only the good and the light, from this status, what can you tell me about my situation and the pain I experience now?"*

And the answer is always, *"Let it be, then let it go"*.

Agree to be with the pain. Don't fight it. And for sure, don't push it away. Don't judge yourself about how you should deal with it. Just be how you feel.

By doing this, you allow yourself to grow through the pain. Then, let it go. Keep growing, keep moving, and keep your heart open. That's the way time helps heal everything.

Sometimes, though, before we find the right person, we have relationships with people that don't work. This is painful. But I promise that every relationship you have will serve to help you and the other person in some way. Nothing is without meaning.

It's almost like you are floating on a pool's surface, and in the bottom of the pool sits a gold coin. In order to reach the coin, you have to 'fall' to the bottom to gain the gold coin.

Every time your heart is broken, you stretch your heart, and it becomes bigger. It's a muscle, and like any muscle, the more you exercise it, the stronger it becomes. And your reward, your *'gold coin'*, is an increased capacity to love. What a gift.

Also, remember my darling, my love, if anyone hurts you, lies to you, manipulates you, or plays with your heart, he will need to deal with me.

In the night, I will go in front of him and crash symbols together on either side of his head. When nobody is watching, I will pee in his garden. I will go to his car and let the air out of his tyres, and from his bicycle tyres, too. I will kidnap his cat, just for a few days (don't worry, I will feed it and make sure to rub its tummy) and then bring it back. I will wear a white sheet and stand in front of his bed in the middle of the night, and whisper to him until he shits the bed.

Above all, I'll be with you. A broken heart is an awful thing, I know. But it will heal in time, believe me.

Focus on your joy and make new goals in your life, because something amazing will come into your life. But how can we recognize this when it happens? (and I know what you're thinking, how the fuck do I know, because I haven't found it… yet).

But even though I believe that the most important thing is to love ourselves unconditionally. We can always love ourself more.

The purpose of life is not to find someone, it's first to find ourself. And I believe that time on Earth is not equal to our time in the Universe. Everyone has a different story, in different times, but when the right person for us arrives, I believe it should feel familiar and natural, almost like a brother would. To love without judgment.

The one that can see your light, your beauty, your worth. Someone to take the time to know you. Someone who cares about you, and loves by his actions, not just words. Someone with whom you can talk for hours and still be interesting and full. Someone who supports your dreams and loves to know about your experience. Someone who loves people, loves life. Someone who respects your challenges and your past. And most of all, someone who accepts you, just as you are.

Whatever you are, whoever you are, you need someone who shares your nature, who has a similar soul, a similar core – you'll be attracted to someone who shares your same inner life.

A king feels comfortable hanging out with his equal, another king. Just as a slave will probably be most comfortable in the company of other slaves. In contrast, a king will not feel at home hanging out with a slave, and vice versa.

So if you are a queen in your inner life and someone else is a slave in his, he will never recognize your worth. You need a king.

You need someone who can hold your hand and give you the space to be who you are: an *'Explosion of Love'*.

HEALING

My darling, my sweet love, I don't know when you will read this book that I'm writing for you. However old you are when you do, and you might be twenty-six, or thirty-six, or fifty-five, I want you to do something for me right now. Find a quiet place in your house, in your room, and lay back on your bed. Support your head with a pillow. Close your eyes, gently, and just breathe.

Slowly, slowly, become more aware of your breathing. Be aware of your body, your toes, your feet, and your legs. Feel your hips and your stomach. Your heart. Try to listen to your heart beating. Feel the sensation of your arms, your hands, your fingers, and your lungs--feel how they move up and down. Soften the muscles in your face. Be aware of the area in your mouth, let the stress go.

After everything you have been through in your life, your experiences of the good and the bad, all the things that you did in your life, all the people you associated with, know that nobody in all the world has had the same experience as you. Nobody in the whole world has seen, tasted, or felt what you have so far.

Now, in this moment, my love, when you are relaxed, I would love to introduce you to the biggest healer you will ever meet in your life: You.

I want you to imagine that you are with yourself in the moment that you were born. Take this new baby, which is you, in your own arms. As you hold this baby, you have, of course, already lived so much, and your many experiences have given you unique wisdom. Now you have this one chance to give this baby--you--invaluable advice. Take your time, my love. Tell this baby what she needs to know. Tell her what you know can help her. You are the only one who can give her the best advice. You are the only one who knows her completely. You are the only one who can help yourself. You are the biggest healer you will ever meet in your whole life. Never forget that.

FELIX

My darling, my love, I want you to know about the greatest hero I have ever met.

This hero dealt with his disease in a way that inspired others. I had the honour and the pleasure to meet Felix. I met Felix about three years before he passed away. One of my friends told me about him. At that time, Felix was about forty-three years old, living by himself in a beautiful house in Jaffa. He was one of the top ten mountain climbers in the world before he got a debilitating disease called ALS. My friend explained that all of their mountain climbing friends were helping Felix. She wondered if I would consider helping, too. I said, of course, I would.

ALS, Amyotrophic Lateral Sclerosis (also known as Lou Gehrig's Disease, after the famous baseball player), is a disease that affects nerve cells in the brain and the spinal cord. The connection between the brain and the muscles gets lost. People who get ALS slowly lose the ability to use their own muscles. It starts first with the legs, and then the arms. Unfortunately, everyone with ALS dies because eventually they lose the ability to breathe. There is no cure. Yet.

The first time I met Felix, it was at his house. His house was in a very expensive neighbourhood in Jaffa. I was very impressed by his home--everything was organised, tidy, and clean. The living room looked like a museum. Every wall was decorated with modern pieces of art. It felt like everything that was in the house was selected after very careful consideration and deliberate design.

When I arrived, Felix was sitting in the living room waiting for me. I was surprised when I saw him. I thought I was going to see a sick man, someone unable to move. Instead, I saw a handsome man with the most dazzling smile I have ever seen, welcoming me. Only his hands and arms looked weak. If I hadn't seen him sitting in a wheelchair, I never would have thought he was someone who needed help.

Felix's eyes were dark green. He always wore glasses and had a French beard, meticulously shaped and carefully shaved. He was wearing a hat that day. But the first thing I noticed about Felix was his smile. It was like the Joker from the casino.

I introduced myself. *"Yes, yes,"* Felix replied. *"I heard about you. Thank you so much for coming, Kapara. We're going to be good friends."* Kapara is a Hebrew word that means *"I will give my life for you."* People often use it as slang now, but actually, it's a warm, affectionate word to express deep feelings for someone.

On that first day, I also met Felix's therapist. She worked twenty-four hours a day for him and lived in the apartment at his estate. She was originally from Romania, in her mid-thirties, beautiful, tall, and full of energy. We liked each other immediately.

Felix asked me if I wanted anything to eat or drink. I said I was fine, and then Felix said, *"Let me show you, Talia, a video of me before I got sick."* Felix picked up the remote control. He struggled a little bit with it because the muscles in his hands and arms were weak. I came instinctively to help him, but he insisted on using it himself. *"It's okay, Kapara, as long as I can, I will do it myself. And, you know, I love to take my time."* And he started to laugh. What an amazing attitude, I thought.

After a few minutes, Felix successfully played the movie. I was shocked. In the movie, Felix was climbing Everest. He was so handsome and strong. When he was at the top of the mountain, he hung from a rock by one finger, and all of him was suspended in the air.

"Look at all my muscles!" he said. I drew an imaginary line between the Felix on the TV screen and how he was now. Life can be hilarious sometimes, in an extreme way.

After we watched the video, he said, *"Okay, Kapara, we need to practice how you will lift me. You need to know how to do it, for when we leave the house. So come, stand close to me and open your legs. Put your knees on either side of mine and keep my legs from moving apart. Good. Great! Now put your arms under mine, and hold your hands together behind my back. When you are ready, push your arms and lift me up, but don't let me fall, Kapara, otherwise it will be painful for me."*

I was so scared, but he trusted me. One, two, three, I lifted Felix. I had no idea he was so tall or heavy. Felix was bent over me. *"What now?"* I asked.

"Now put me back on the seat." I did it so quickly, without thinking that he would need me to do it slower.

Felix started to laugh. *"You're great, Talia, but you almost killed me. Next time, just more slowly. Okay? Great, Kapara, let's go out and catch the day!"*

"Where are we going?"

"We're going everywhere."

On that particular day, Felix and I went to the beach first. I stood on the back of his wheelchair while Felix pushed the button on the wheelchair with his finger, and we zoomed fast along the sidewalk. We went to the art gallery to see if there was anything new on, and everyone in the art gallery shop knew him. Apparently, he was a regular visitor there. He bought an expensive saltshaker. I was stunned. I asked him why on earth he paid so much for a saltshaker. *"Who cares,"* he said, laughing. *"I'm going to die, and this shaker makes me feel good."*

Afterwards, we met with a drumming group at the beach, and Felix talked with everyone, all the time laughing and joking. Later, he wanted to go home. He wanted to know when I would come back. *"In a few days,"* I said.

For about a year, I visited Felix two or three times a week. It was always fun and interesting. Sometimes it was also painful. One day I came to visit, and he was trying to brush his teeth with the one finger that was still working. But not anymore. Felix was broken. *"I could do it yesterday,"* he said, and he started to cry. Immediately, he stopped himself and said, *"It's okay. I accept. I'm still alive. I will enjoy every moment. I know this is a temporary situation. Let's go out. Let's have fun."* Straight away, he changed his mood. We stayed out all day, laughing, talking, and singing.

So many people visited Felix every day that it was almost like queuing for an audience with the Pope. So many people came by every day. There was so much love. One day, I asked him why so many people visited. He told me, *"It's very simple. When I got sick, I decided to be as positive as possible. One of the things that makes me happy and keeps me feeling good is having people around. So I give my love to everyone that comes here, and I share my weakness. That's the way I help myself."* He was right. Felix took every situation, no matter how hard or embarrassing, and transformed it into a positive.

Like showering. One evening, Felix asked me to shower him because his therapist was off for the weekend and he needed a shower. It was a little bit embarrassing for me. I was a twenty-six-year-old woman, and he was a forty-three-year-old man. He showed me how. In the bathtub, there was a special seat, and he needed my help to sit on it. I helped him from the wheelchair to the special seat in the bath. Then he explained that I had to undress him. *"The underpants, too, Kapara. I can't have a shower with them on."*

When I took off his underpants, he said, *"You see, Kapara, I may be sick, but I am a complete man!"* I filled the bath, and he directed me to soap him. He laughed at how he looked and joked that he looked like an idiot because of his hands. He laughed like it was the end of the world. *"Don't forget my ass,"* he said. And then, playfully, he added, *"What can I do? I can't reach."* I forgot my embarrassment completely and laughed, too.

Sometime later, on another one of my visits, Felix and I were out, and I asked him, *"Felix, what has this disease given you?"* He said, *"It's the best thing that has ever happened to me... if I become healthy again."*

"Why?"

"Because this disease has helped me become who I am. I see people in a different way."

Felix had the spirit of a fighter. No matter what his physical condition was, he never gave up. He almost convinced himself that his condition was temporary and that he could change. After all, people with the same disease often lived only two or three years, whereas he was already in his fifth year with the disease. Before Felix got his disease, he was one of the top 10 mountain climbers in the world. He would climb at least three or four times a week. It was his passion, love, and adventure. For him, getting this disease and having to stop climbing was as painful as it would be for Mozart to lose his ability to create music. I'm not exaggerating here. And yet instead of focusing on his losses, he chose to dwell on the positive. Instead of feeling sorry or mad because life was unfair, he turned his heart toward the joy that can be found in every life, in every circumstance.

Felix used to go to ALS meetings. Listening to everyone's stories gave him power and inspiration. He and a few mountain-climbing friends decided to raise awareness of ALS and raise money for the study and cure of the disease. Together, they built a special machine that would enable Felix to climb the tallest building in Tel Aviv, Israel, by pulling on a rope. Felix went on a morning radio show and spoke about his disease to advertise the climb. The event was filmed and aired on national TV. For Felix, this event was a big day and a huge achievement. He missed being high up. Without special assistance, he couldn't do it.

He asked me so many times why I didn't climb mountains. He said it was such fun and that I didn't know what I was missing. He vowed that when he was healthy, he would work out in the gym twenty-four hours a day until he was as fit as he used to be. He knew it would take a long time to get fit again, but he never let go of that hope, no matter how impossible it might seem.

Sometimes I wondered if Felix knew how little time he actually had, or if it was just the way he kept himself positive. He couldn't ignore the medical situation that was becoming worse and worse. We went to see a medical doctor to see if he could improve Felix's breathing. Felix tested his breath with a machine, and although he tried to breathe as deeply as he could, the result of the test showed his breathing capacity was shockingly low. Also, when he sneezed, he sounded like an old British lady from the 17th Century, drinking tea, with a bee on her nose. Felix joked about himself all the time.

One day, I got a call from him asking where I was. His therapist was away for the weekend, and I had volunteered to be with him, but I was running late. *"Hurry up!"* he said. *"I really need to go to the toilet."*

I rushed as fast as I could. When I got to his place and saw him sitting there and waiting for me, I felt terrible. After I took him to the toilet, I heated up some food for him and fed him. He scolded and teased me. *"Do you mind mixing the mashed potato with the corn a little bit? It's very boring to eat just one thing at a time. The fun is having a mixture in the mouth."* Every time I brought the fork near his mouth, Felix would turn his head or make a funny face and make it into a big joke.

"Kapara," he said. *"I need to ask you something else. Can you see that book over there? On the second shelf? Can you straighten the book, please?"* I got up and pointed to the one he spoke about. I straightened it. He asked me to fix up another one, the fifth book on the third shelf. And then again, another one on the third shelf, the fifth book from the left.

"Enough, Felix!" I shouted. *"You're making me crazy! Try to live in peace when not all your books stand like soldiers in the army."*

"Okay, okay. Don't be hard on me."

"I'm not, but don't drive me crazy!"

"Talia, you know, this disease has changed me so much. Before, I was only concerned about myself. And just to think how I was with women! You can't imagine how many women I had. I think about it now, and wow, I was such an idiot! Do you know what I did? I numbered them in a list and wrote down who was the best in bed. I could cry about it now."

"Felix," I said. *"It doesn't matter how you were. It matters only who you are now."*

Evening came, and Felix started yawning like a hippo in a pool. We went to his bedroom. I lifted him from the wheelchair to the bed and sat him up. When he was on the bed, he asked me to open the closet. Everything was so incredibly tidy, like artifacts in a museum. *"Your therapist works very hard, huh?"* I said. *"Are you trying to make her crazy?"*

He laughed. *"No. You know we have an amazing friendship."*

"Yes, I noticed that," I said.

He directed me to a pair of pajamas on the left side of the cupboard, with black squares. I pointed. *"Yes, that's the one."* I moved to take the pajamas, and Felix lost his balance and fell over onto his right side on the bed.

"Aha, faster Kapara!"

"Okay, okay." Dressing Felix, I had to be faster, too.

"No, no, not the hands first. The head first. Hello! Here I am!"

First the right hand, then the left. Then his pants, and for that, we had to lift him up again a bit. After he was dressed in pajamas, I straightened him on the bed as he asked and covered him with the blanket. I turned on the nightlight, and he asked for a goodnight kiss. *"Can I ask you for a favour?"* he asked.

"Of course."

"Can you scratch my nose, please?"

I scratched his nose.

"But Felix," I said. *"What will you do if you have to move in the middle of the night, or go to the toilet?"*

"Don't worry," Felix said. *"I will wake you up."*

"How? Don't tell me you can walk at night. I'm starting to think you are pretending to be sick."

"Haha, I got you." Felix laughed. *"I wish I could. I will just call you or scream. Please come if I do, Kapara."*

"So that's it? You're just going to sleep?" I felt sadness in my heart. That he wouldn't move all night, and yet there he was, with a smile on his face.

I went to the other room to sleep, leaving his light on for him. I changed my clothes by myself, lay on the bed by myself, scratched my nose by myself. What a privilege it is to scratch your own nose whenever you feel like it.

"Felix!" I yelled from the other room. *"Are you okay?"*

"What, Kapara? I just fell asleep!"

"I thought maybe you wanted to scratch your nose."

"No, thank you. Good night."

I thought to myself, he never complains, he really accepts his situation. What an amazing person he is.

"Hey Felix," I shouted out. *"Do you need to go to the toilet?"*

"Kapara, you woke me up again! No, thank you, I don't need to go to the toilet."

"Okay, okay, sorry!" I thought to myself, we are all locked in our own body, but Felix is locked twice. It's like being buried in the ground when you are still alive.

"Felix!" I called again. *"Are you okay? Do you want to change sides?"*

"Kapara, Enough! It's the third time you've woken me up now. You are fired!" We both burst out laughing. After a while, he said, *"Don't feel sad about me. Come and give me another kiss and then we'll go to sleep, okay?"* I went to Felix and hugged him so hard. *"Don't kill me, please,"* he said. I kissed him again and went to sleep. Felix didn't wake me up even one time.

In the morning, we waited for Felix's therapist, but she didn't come back. Felix said to me that he thought she had left for good.

"Whoa. Why would you say that?"

"Look at her room, it's empty. She will not come back."

"But I thought you were good friends."

"Yes, we are. But maybe it got too hard for her."

"Maybe you are right."

She never came back.

Felix was very sad. But he found another therapist. When I was overseas, I heard that he had also found love. I was happy for him.

To be with Felix, you feel the pressure of time, running away like sand through an hourglass.

Those times when I saw Felix and the way he was, I saw someone who appreciated every moment. Someone who kept himself up and very positive. I saw someone who chose to be a hero, not a victim. After all, his circumstances were so hard and dramatic, and the reality of death was present all of the time. He could have chosen to be very sad, depressed, angry, and bitter. Nobody would have judged him for that, but the way Felix was is a reminder for all of us. You might not have control of your circumstances. But you can be the master of your attitude. And because Felix was a master of positive attitude, he didn't just help himself, but he took everyone up with him.

It was fun and light to be around him. He didn't have one second of sorrow. You loved him more, and your heart opened more when you saw how he dealt with this disease.

Anytime when I find myself down or want to complain, I remember Felix. And I will carry him in my heart all of my life. Almost, I can see him, with his big smile, whisper into my ear, *"Kapara: why are you complaining? Enjoy life! Because our attitude changes every aspect of our life--when we choose to be positive!"*

Felix is an amazing example of the power we have when we have a positive attitude.

The last time I saw Felix was the time I decided to leave Israel. We were sitting in a beautiful cafe.

"I need to talk with you, Felix. I'm moving from Israel."

"For how long?"

"For a long time." Felix looked at me with sadness in his face.

"So it's the last time we're going to see each other."

"Probably yes."

Felix looked at me, and there was quiet between us. I didn't know what to say. It was the longest minute in all my life.

"I need to ask you something, Kapara.'

"Ask me anything," I said.

"Tell my story."

TIME

Into the sun,

An abundance of love,

Play with a kite,

Form of God.

In mama earth, I play with my drum.

What is that between both of us?

Only time.

WHEN YOU ARE DOWN

My sweet, sweet darling, my love, my only one, it's okay to feel down. We all have times like that in life. But please don't be too hard on yourself. Don't judge yourself. It's okay to make mistakes. We all do. Tomorrow is a new day, a new beginning. You can fix anything with honesty. Be loyal to yourself. And if you think you did something wrong, forgive yourself. First of all, you are a human being. It takes strength to apologise. Life is a training exercise, not a test.

You did something, and you failed? Good on you that you tried! Try again. My love, the most important thing is the way you do something, not the achievement of your goal. Don't give up. You have everything you need inside yourself. Use it. Bring out all the good that is inside. You are good, smart, beautiful, fantastic, amazing, more than you think you are.

Someone said something critical about you? Someone hurt you? Does it feel right? Does it feel true? Be honest with yourself. Ask yourself, from where does this person talk? Is he like an angel in your life, showing you something about yourself that you may need to let go of, or is he talking from his own fear or frustration? If he were like an angel, bless him and listen carefully. This is a chance to overcome some block inside yourself. If he is not, brush his words from yourself and let them go. You are not a garbage bin for someone else's negativity.

Has someone turned their back on you? Good, let him go. He's not worthy of you. It may be hard to see that now, but in a while, something much better will come your way. So let them go. Goodbye, bye, bye.

If someone lies to you, and you are being honest, the lies stay with him. Not with you. Unfortunately, his personality will become full of lies. Whoever lies goes with lies. You will never experience regret as long as you are being honest: whoever is honest goes with honesty.

Are you feeling alone? Do you feel rejection from friends? There are so many options in life. There are so many people. If you don't feel comfortable in some situations, trust your feelings, my love. Trust your first instinct. Don't stay there, move on. If you don't feel you can be who you are, it's not the right situation for you. The universe holds infinite possibilities for you. Trust that you will come down where you are meant to be.

You feel like crying? It's okay, my love, let it out. It's healthy to express feelings. Don't stop yourself, my beautiful darling. Take your time to be sad. Every child who falls stops to cry, but when they are done, they continue. Don't fall in love with pain; let it go.

The best thing, my love, is to talk with God. Find some quiet place and just say what you are feeling, as if you are talking with a best friend. I promise you that something will always happen. It's like magic. You are never alone, my love, never. You know, my love, that I am here for you, always, unconditionally. If you want to talk with me, I'm here. Even if we've had an argument. My love and support for you is forever and to infinity.

If you feel like talking to your friends, talk to those who love you. But if I can give you advice, my darling, look for the friends with the eyes of birds. They are the ones who can see the big picture.

It goes like this: always seek advice from those who can understand you and your life. If you are a Rabbi, seek advice from a Rabbi. If you are a hooker, seek advice from a hooker. (But don't be a rabbi who seeks advice from a hooker.)

Remember, you are never alone. You are an abundance of love. You are the creation of love. A one-time traveller in the world. You have your own music in your soul, sing it. Keep going, my love. Life is too short to be stuck.

You don't like how you look? You compare yourself to other women? The giraffe never compares itself to the elephant! Go to the mirror, look at yourself. This is Art. You are art. Nobody in all the world looks like you. You are beautiful, my love, unique and special. You put five kilos on?

It suits you, my love; you need to look like you. You have pimples on your face? Let it be. It will go in time. Nobody will even notice.

You feel bored and stuck with life? That's fantastic. Something in you wants to go out. Hold on, because very soon change is coming.

You don't know what you want? It's okay, my love. You don't have to know everything. You have all the time in the world to figure it out. Just be cool about not knowing. Don't take yourself so seriously, darling. Laugh about yourself. Say something good about yourself. Say out loud: I am good, I am great, I am wonderful, just because I am who I am. I love, and I bring love everywhere.

Is someone criticising you? Are they telling stories about you that aren't true? Have you found yourself in the courts being blamed for something that you did not do? Listen carefully, darling. If you sit in the house and watch TV every day for hours, like a potato chip, nobody will bother you. If you are busy and active, if you allow yourself to be successful and beautiful, as you are, then someone will wake up to you. But would you really rather be a safe potato chip when you are meant to be a brilliant shooting star? There is nothing new under the sun. The more you do, the more criticism you will get. This is a good sign. It means that you are doing a lot of work in this world. Keep going. Don't let anyone stop you from bringing good into the world. Rise above the jealousy of others, and don't let anybody pull you down.

Did you create something? Are you looking for a job? Or maybe for an opportunity? You get a lot of rejection? That's great, my darling. The more No's you get, the stronger the Yes will be. Keep knocking on the doors! One day, not just a door, but a huge gate will be opened for you.

My Darling, do you find yourself waiting ages? Does life require you to wait patiently for the next chapter? It is not in your hands to speed this process up. I'm impressed, my darling. You are going to become a very wise woman. The more you wait for something, the brighter you will become. The music happens in the quiet space between the notes. If things come quickly to your path, you will not have the chance to see how the Creator works. If life makes you sit down and wait, you will start to learn how God is present in every single moment of this life.

So, my darling, my love, are you stressed about money? (Well, you can always rob a bank!) This can be very stressful.

Do something for me right now. Close your eyes and put your right hand on your heart; listen to mum. In this moment–right now–in your life, not tomorrow, not another three weeks. Now.

In this moment, is something missing in your life? You have a roof over your head? Food in your fridge? Or perhaps not. It doesn't matter. In this moment, everything is as it should be. Trust this moment, my love, and all that you do have. Your money situation can change very quickly. The more you trust this moment, the more money will come to your life. At this moment, nothing is missing.

Always find ways to lift your spirit up.

Buy the dress in the shop, even if you are short of money. Put music on, dance, and sing, even if your voice sounds like a sick cat. Show the world the best smile you have, and bring the love in your heart out for the world to see. Love yourself, my darling. Nobody in the world can love you more than you love yourself. Be sure you are surrounded with your loving friends, often. Spread the love. Tidy up your room, it will clear your mind. Light aromatherapy candles. Choose a positive statement that you can repeat to yourself, something like: *'I have everything I need. I am surrounded by an abundance of love.'* Say it a thousand times until you convince yourself. Put flowers in your room. Make a new goal. It could be to learn another language. Go out to the park, write a list of all the good things you have in life. Remember, my darling. We all feel down sometimes in our life. And then we go through these situations and come up stronger and wiser. It's part of life; we will experience it through our hearts. Emotion is like the ocean, like waves in the sea; they come and go. But the sea always exists and liberates. Keep going, my love, and serve in the ocean of life.

And always remember, there's calm after the storm.

You are beautiful as you are. You just need to let your beauty and love out and agree to be who you are.

You are bigger than you think you are. You are blessed and loved, an *'Explosion of Love'*.

Bless you, my love.

CHOOSING THE POSITIVE

My love, my darling, my only one, in life you have two options: to laugh or to cry. If you cry, at some point, you need to stop. If you choose to laugh, you will find more reasons to laugh, especially at yourself. To choose laughter and positivity is actually art in action. I have a friend who specializes in this, always choosing positivity, no matter what. I'm happy to tell you about Abby.

Abby is one of my flatmates. My friendship with Abby developed slowly, but the interesting thing is that it continues going in one direction, deeper and deeper.

Today, not a single day passes without Abby and me talking for over an hour. Our favourite conversation is about life. What else is there to talk about but the meaning and the blessings in life? And our views of the world and the people who surround us. Abby is the same age as me, thirty-six years old. She's a Kiwi who grew up on a farm. She's very tall--180 cm--and as thin as the stick of a mop. She has brown eyes and a big, beautiful smile. She dresses differently every day. The hair above one of her ears is shaved, and the skin on her face is scarred by acne. She welcomes everyone with a big smile on her face, and her opening words are always: *"Hello, beautiful. Hello, darling!"*

When you talk with Abby, it almost feels as if she is sitting in the corner of the conversation and waiting for the first opportunity to jump in and start to laugh. She really takes her time with a laugh, enjoying every moment of it. When you see her room, you feel you are visiting Alice in Wonderland; it's so wild and beautiful.

When I talk about positivity in action, what I mean is you have a choice. That choice is about deciding how to deal with difficulty. You will find that once you make a decision, you empower yourself. You are not a victim anymore, but you start to become a leader. Until you make a choice, it is like you are riding a horse without reins, but when you make a decision, the horse's reins are in your hands.

Abby has learned this secret, and it has transformed her life. She shared it with me one day.

"You know, darling, I haven't always been happy. I used to suffer very badly from anxiety. I had so many fears, I was sure I would die young. I was so afraid of everything, it felt like my heart was exploding from my chest. It would feel almost like I was having a heart attack or a panic attack."

"So what did you do? How did you become the woman you are today?"

"Well," Abby said to me. *"I did a lot of work on myself. Spiritual work. My Mum started reading spiritual books and recommended them to me. So I read all of them. Because I'm a*

perfectionist, I followed all of the advice and the exercises the books recommended. I read a hundred books, if not more. At some point, I felt like I had graduated, and I knew it was working. I learned so much. I understood that it was my choice and my responsibility to be happy. That I am the one who controls how to deal with what I feel. Now, I feel ashamed if I say I'm sad or depressed, because in my opinion, I can only blame myself. If I feel bad, I need to do something about it rather than sink into the feeling. It's not that I don't still have the feeling that my heart is going to explode and that it's hard to breathe. I still do. But what I tell myself now has changed. I tell myself that what I'm feeling is excitement, that it's not bad."

Abby is a talented makeup artist. She said to me one day, *"You know, darling, I feel so blessed to do the work I do. I love it. I love to make people feel good about themselves. This job gives me the opportunity to be close to people, working with brides, models, and actors on the sets of movies. My favourite way to make up people is always to keep their natural look. The secret is to wear makeup, but look like you aren't wearing any. You know, darling, today the attitude about beauty is so fake, it makes me laugh. All the treatments people use to cover up their age. What's wrong with looking old if you are old? All the Botox that people put on their face means they can't express their feelings. They cry, but they can't move."*

I agree with Abby. Today, the attitude towards beauty from magazines and TV shows favours one format of beauty.

It's like everyone should look the same. The media puts attention on the beauty outside, but doesn't focus on the beauty that is inside. All of us women, all the time, want to change something about how we look. We are never pleased with how we look, thinking that if we lose five kilos, or have longer hair, we would look better. We could continue with this forever, until we make a decision. Listen to what Abby says about this.

"You know, darling, when I was young, I truly thought I was ugly. When I was a teenager, I started to get acne on my face, I suffered about this so much. But one day, I met a lady in her forties in the pharmacy. She had skin like mine. I saw how much she suffered because of it. I could see how stuck she was, trapped in her negative thinking. It woke me up and lit a red light inside myself. I decided that I didn't want to be like her. So, on that day, I decided to live in peace with my skin and never be bothered about it anymore. That's it. I love myself with the skin on my face."

Abby is right. When you meet her, you see a beautiful, tall woman with a gorgeous smile and eyes. Who cares about her skin when there's such an abundance of beauty that she gives? Because she doesn't give attention to it, nobody else cares.

Positivity in action is something that when you use it once, you learn to use it more. One day, Abby met a man named Jonathon through her friends. It was so exciting.

Jonathon came over for about three or four months, and it felt and looked right, but then he came over less and less, until he disappeared. Abby was broken with disappointment. It was hard for me to hear one of her conversations with her father. *"I feel rejected and poor."* She cried and cried.

But we are talking here about someone who takes responsibility for her actions. So Abby used her wisdom to go back to the positive. Every morning, she wrote positive messages to herself. She dressed up as if she were promoting a Hollywood movie. She made herself look the best she could. She caught up with lots of friends, and she travelled. She told me, *"You know, darling, I'm not angry anymore with Jonathon. It happened. When you think you like someone but he doesn't have the same feelings towards you, it can be very painful.*

But you don't get a guarantee that the one you like will like you the same. And even if it's like that in the beginning, it can change. People are allowed to change their mind, and their feelings. And I learnt to respect that and not to feel so down about this subject.

I don't think Jonathon is a bad person, and I don't think or feel that he lied or played with my heart. He just didn't like me as he thought, and I'm learning to let it go and to put more focus and love on myself.

I feel like I'm growing spiritually. I'm back to the game."

I don't remember how long after this, maybe five or six months, Abby came back from Raglan and told me, *"Guess what, darling? I met a sweet, sweet boy named Adrian, and tonight I'm going to have dinner and sex with him."*

Well, my darling, a year later, Abby is still having dinner and sex with this sweet, sweet boy. Abby told me, *"You know, I feel he's made for me. It's so easy to be with him; he's such a gorgeous person. He fits into my life perfectly. For me, it's good that it started with sex because I didn't have expectations."*

I'm so happy for Abby. They are a truly blessed couple.

To be friends with Abby and see how she reacts to the world can make every flower blossom. For me, Abby is the epitome of the Art of Positivity. This Art is twenty-four-hours-a-day work because life, all the time, challenges us. We can easily subconsciously or consciously choose to be upset from the circumstances we experience in life. But the good news is that we have power. For us to choose positivity might seem too hard. After all, we are so weak, all of us, we can so easily lose our balance quickly when we do not get what we want, or if we are surrounded by people who feel down. But when we remind ourselves that we can choose to be positive and take action to avoid falling down, we empower ourselves. And to be an Artist is to be good and positive first and foremost to yourself.

I'm blessed and grateful for Abby's presence in my life because when I'm with her and see how she takes care of her positive attitude, it inspires me to do the same.

It's like this, my darling: The people who surround you-- if they are positive--will encourage you to be positive. The people who choose negativity will take you down with them. Be sure, my darling, that you surround yourself with positive people, to encourage you to be as you are.

An *'Explosion of Love!'*

FATE

My darling, my love, my sweet love, the way I see life is that it is a big opportunity to really become who you are. Here is a truth I have come to understand: To become who you are, you have to find a way to connect to your spirituality and to accept that we are all part of The One, God.

We do that not just by saying it, but by feeling it in the deepest part of our soul. I have a belief that we are not alone here. We are moving in the backyard of God. We are like a baby that moves in the womb of his mother. The baby doesn't see his mother, but she surrounds him and feeds him, she is his sponsor.

In my opinion, all of our problems in the world, all of our weaknesses and illnesses, come from the same roots: that we are not truly connected to the source of God. We feel rejection from somewhere. We feel hurt. It's like when a baby is delivered from the womb, and the doctor cuts the umbilical cord. The baby feels separate from his own mother, the one who created him. He feels alone. It has taken me a long time to feel comfortable and to understand that God is here, close inside and out. For me, religion talks about God with rules and conditions and takes God far away from me. Once I started to feel and accept that God is inside me, I felt close to my own navel. Close to my own real voice, the high spiritual one.

There are so many questions, so many doubts about God. Why do we have war in the world? Where is God? Why do good people suffer so much? How could the Holocaust happen? Where was God then? If He can do everything, if He is the high level of light, why didn't He do something? Why did He let that happen? Where is justice in this world? So many struggle to find understanding. To see the meaning and pattern of their lives. To know their purpose and find joy in it. I do believe, my darling, that this world is based on choice. Choice is the fundamental element of this world. It's like your own body can't function without oxygen; life is stifled without the ability to choose.

You can choose to bring your light out and be guided by it, or you can choose to use your fear so that darkness will be in your actions. That's the essential element of this world: our power to choose light or dark, hope or despair, love or hate. If I were to put it into black and white, you can choose God, or not. I believe that God gives us this ability and this power. Each of us is part of God. If we choose Him, we bring Him out into the world. We reflect the light, the good, the love.

So if a lot of people choose God inside themselves, the power of good will increase in the world. If people do not choose for good, then the power of darkness takes control instead. God is so big He can't present all of Himself in one piece. He needs us. So He makes Himself a home inside of each of us, a piece of Him in each of us. When one person chooses God and brings out the light, he changes the atmosphere. Now, if more people would choose God, the world and reality will also change. Then we will not need to fight because we will have peace inside ourselves. When we love ourselves, then we can love others.

When we accept who we are, we will be more patient with our weaknesses and more patient with others. Sometimes people ask me: *"Are you Jewish? Then you are chosen by God. Really? And you are not chosen by God?"*

I believe God chooses everyone. It is we who do not choose God. I do believe it happens in history that groups of people choose God. Through this choice, they become *'chosen by God'*. So they have chosen. It is a bit like God invites everyone to a big party. Everyone is welcome, but not everyone accepts the invitation. The invitation remains open, but some people never accept. Choosing God is not a one-time thing; it's an ongoing choice we make over and over. Life is full of gifts and wonderful surprises. But life also liberally sprinkles ugly and unfair things along our path. Like Bertie Bott's Every Flavor Jelly Beans, we never quite know if we'll get something delightful or rather hideous. Even the strongest spirits will eventually need some help and support. We need something strong inside us; we need a connection to find this shining, bright, pureness from inside and bring it out. I do believe that if all of us will choose the light, we will all feel inter-connected, existing in a unified consciousness, like one big human being. The world will be different.

I have to say to you, my darling, there was an amazing time in my life when I had the honour to work with many people before they passed away. I noticed something similar about everyone: before the end, everyone realized that God existed. The people who felt they hadn't made the right choices earlier had so many regrets. Why run a marathon only to realize just at the end that you were running the opposite way?

I also started to notice that there is justice in this world, spiritual justice. Justice is not just something that you can see on the surface; it happens inside the body, inside the soul. I do believe that between the struggling of the ego and the soul, the soul is always stronger. If someone turns their back on their soul, their soul forces them to face it in the end. I believe the purpose of life is to update our soul. The soul is the only thing that is left after we die, and God wants that piece of him back. I can't see myself living without this feeling of connection and love. This is my real oxygen. If I lose this feeling, I will fall for the illusion of this world, and fear will take control of me.

In this book written for you, I have one strong message to tell you: Believe in your inner feelings. Even if the outside reality doesn't seem to match them. I believe that true reality is inside, never outside.

PATIENCE

My darling, my love, my only one, in life, all of us need a lot of patience. What helped me to deal with patience is to understand that it's all about timing.

Let me tell you a story about patience. When I was young, I really wanted a cat. That was my dream of dreams. I couldn't imagine anything better. A white one, with blue eyes. I ached for a cat. My room was covered in pictures of cats. But in our house, we always had dogs.

I waited and hoped for what felt like an eternity. Maybe ten years passed, but I never asked specifically for a cat. I just knew that somehow, someday my dream would appear. But I didn't expect to have to wait so long, so patiently for it.

I was around seventeen years old when our dog Nicki died. My father didn't want us to have another pet. He said, *"I don't want to hear a word about having another pet at home."*

One night, I had a dream. I dreamed that in the morning, a cat would come to our home. Now, I had no idea how this would happen, but when I opened my eyes from this dream, I went straight downstairs without thinking and opened the front door.

We lived in a building with five levels. The entrance to the building is locked. I opened the front door of our flat, and I couldn't believe what I was seeing. In front of me was a cat. It was a white cat with a long tail and long whiskers. It didn't have blue eyes, but it had brown eyes with yellow flecks, like a gypsy cat. She looked at me, and it was as if she said, *"Hello to you. I came to you from your dream. Meouw."*

Whoa! I was so, so happy. I couldn't believe it.

My mum and my brother came to see what all the excitement was about. *"Wow, how did this cat get in?"*

"She came to me. I dreamed about this. I don't care Mum, she has to stay, okay. Okay?"

"But what will we do with your Dad?" said my Mum. *"You know what? I have an idea. We will hide her. When Dad gets home from work, we will put the cat in Daniels's room. Do you agree, Daniel?"*

My brother agreed. *"Good idea, Mum."*

"And when Dad leaves the house in the morning, we will let her walk free in the house. It will be our secret."

I named my cat Beatrice. Evening came, and my father arrived from work. We hid Beatrice in my brother's room. We ate dinner together before moving to the living room to watch the news. Then the worst thing happened. Beatrice, my cat, walked from my brother's room straight into the living room. She walked in as if she were some Bohemian from Saint Gallize, or a Versace model, with her tail straight up in the air. She stopped directly in front of my father, and looked at him in such a way that it was like she said, *"Hi. I'm Beatrice, the cat in the house. What are you going to do about it? Meouw."*

My father was shocked. His eyes wide, he pointed at the cat. *"What is that?"* We were quiet.

My mum said, *"Talia, what is that?"*

I replied, *"I don't know."*

My brother said, *"It's a strange creature."*

My mum said, *"Yes, it's very strange. It has a tail and a moustache. It's a very strange creature."*

"Ah! I know what it is!" said my brother. "This is a giraffe."

My father said to my Mum, *"Ketzi?"* Ketzi is my mother's nickname, which means *'cat'* in Yiddish.

My Mum said, *"This is an elephant."*

"No, no," said my brother. *"It's a monkey."*

"Okay! ENOUGH! This is a cat, you see? A cat," I said. My cat Beatrice turned her head immediately and looked at me as if she would say, *"Play tough, huh.... Push him! Meouw."*

I got her message and continued to talk with my Dad.

"This is my cat," I said. *"She came to me from a dream. Now you have two options. Option one: the cat stays in the house. Option two: I leave the house with the cat. What is your decision?"*

My father started to laugh. *"You are not leaving the house, young lady. And the cat stays. You had lots of patience."*

I was so happy. I had a very strong connection with Beatrice. Every day when I came home, she would follow me around like a dog.

After a year, she left as suddenly as she had come.

And I accepted that without qualm, with a peaceful heart. Our story was finished, and I was lucky enough to have her for the time we had been together. After all, she came like a gift that fell from the sky for me. As a reward for all of my years that I wished and waited patiently for the cat. It was enough that she had joined me on my journey for a while.

I find that patience is a common theme in my life, and sometimes the limit of my patience is stretched so long and so high that I struggle with this. Again. And again. But then I remember my cat, Beatrice. Looking back, I realized that only when I left the obsession to have a cat and to continue with my life with faith, that the universe fulfilled my wish, and I trust that the universe will continue to provide for me at the perfect time all good things that I hope for and dream of.

Because of this, I have a lot of patience inside of me, which is the biggest treasure you can give yourself. It calms your emotions and relaxes your mind. Patience makes all good things sweeter once they come into your life, and fills your heart with hope while you are waiting.

In Hebrew, the word patience is *'savlanoot'*, and the root of this word is *'sevel'*, which means to suffer. In time, when life requires us to be patient, it involves suffering. Especially when we lose our patience. When we doubt that we'll get what we want, we lose trust; it's hard, and we suffer.

But when we trust, and at the same time let go, we come to understand that timing is the key. And we know that the universe will give us what we really need, for the universe knows better than us when the right time will be. It is then that patience becomes another word for 'timing'. And when we know that, we can let go of our fears and worries, and live in calm assurance that all good things come to those who wait.

INTO THE SCHOOL

My lovely darling, in life, it doesn't matter what you get. It matters who you meet. There are people who hold the flag and the torch; they know the way. They are guides. It's easy to recognise them because they touch your deepest heart. You will never forget them, and they will empower you. I had one teacher like that. I adored him.

I'm proud to declare that I was one of the students of Moshe Gardus. When I was sixteen years old, I was in high school. The classes were separated into subjects, and you were only admitted if your grades were good enough. I wasn't a good student. I desperately wanted to get into the psychology class or into the literature class, but the only class I was accepted into was bookkeeping. I decided to give bookkeeping a try, and hoped I would like it. Well, darling, I tried, but it didn't work. I hated it. I was so bored in school, and my grades were so low that at the end of the year, they wanted me to repeat it. I thought, "What?! This nightmare, again?"

At around the same time, I heard a lot of stories about a private school called Ancory. A lot of the stories were especially about the director and educator, Moshe Gardus. The stories gave me such a good feeling that I wanted to study there. I decided to talk to my parents about it. I told them that my school wanted me to repeat the year, and I didn't want to. My father told me that he had a friend who had been forced to repeat a year, and he said, *"Talia, it was terrible for him, and I don't want you to go through it. We will send you to Ancory, even if it costs a lot of money."* I appreciated that so much. Going to Ancory was one of my best decisions.

Ancory Rishon Lezion was a small school, actually just on a single level with only around ten classrooms. There was an office, Gardus' room, a school counsellor's room, and a teachers' lounge. Downstairs, there was a small outside area with a single bench where we were allowed to smoke. Gardus' attitude was, *"I know you are smoking cigarettes, I don't need you to hide it from me. You can smoke freely outside."*

When I started school at Ancory, I felt as free as a bird. There was something in the air that allowed you to be who you should be. The school's focus was to give you the tools you needed to be a better person. It was about interests and aptitudes, not about scores. In the teachers' meetings, they talked about our personalities, not about our achievements.

MOSHE GARDUS, THE MAN AND THE LEGEND

I think Moshe Gardus was nearly forty years old when I first met him. He was around 173 cm tall, with slanting brown eyes full of intelligence and life. When he looked at you, it felt like he was looking into your soul. Most of the time, he wore a buttoned shirt, and he had a small belly. His hands were energetic, moving all the time. He wore glasses and, of course, had the familiar habit of moving the glasses up to the top of his nose with one finger every three seconds. He had a bushy beard and thinning brown hair. Style, like Santa Claus. He was always so busy and moved quickly. He couldn't wait. He had a mission, and it was very clear to him. His mission was to deliver educational value to everyone in the school and to always be aware of how they were feeling. His office looked more like that of a teenage rock star, with funny pictures everywhere and a plastic water pistol that he liked to shoot us with whenever he felt like it. His office door was always open, and you were always welcome if you needed to talk to him or just be there.

In my second year at Ancory, I finally got to be in Gardus' class for psychology and sociology. The way Moshe Gardus taught us was very clear: *"I will give you everything, teach you everything, based on honesty. You have to listen to me and do your homework. If not, I will punish you as creatively as I wish. I will take care to keep you focused."* And, yes, Gardus knew how to do that. He loved to call us by our surname and sometimes by our nicknames. I was *"Shefinka."*

If someone was late to the class, their punishment was to find 100 bottle caps outside and to name each one. The requirement for sociology was to have a bright yellow marker. You must have it. *"Ah, you forgot yours? By tomorrow morning, you will write a love song to your marker and read it out in front of the class."*

Gardus' classes could be unpredictable. In the middle of the class, someone would be asked to read an article out loud. Gardus would pace excitedly, back and forth, to the front and to the back of the room. Then, when Gardus recognized a very important line, he would repeat it loudly. Running to the blackboard, he would write the statement in big letters and say to everyone, *"Markers in the air in your right hand and now... highlight it in your books!"* Or, if he ever saw someone daydreaming, he would walk to their desk and BAM! He would slam his hand on their desks to get their attention. Sometimes he would tie a boy's shoelaces together. Or he might sit on your desk.

One morning, he came to the class and looked at me. *"Are you okay?"* he asked me. Before I had a chance to answer, he said, *"Okay, everyone out. You, Talia, come to my office."*

"Tell me, Talia, what is bothering you?"

"Nothing."

"Are you sure?" he asked. *"You know you can always talk to me."*

On this day, nothing was bothering me, but the fact that he was concerned touched my heart.

There was a deep sense of security that came from knowing Gardus had our best interests in mind, even when that meant a little *'tough love.'* When Gardus had a meeting with all the students one day, he pointed someone out. *"Yes, you, stand up. I saw you in the morning driving, and you didn't stop when you should have stopped. Do you know what that means? Do you understand the consequences of your actions?"* Gardus would call the parents straight away to report if students had done something wrong. His mission was to help us become the best people we could be, in every facet of life.

One day, one of the students in our class called to say that he was sick. For a whole week, he did not come to school. When he returned, it was clear that he had not been sick, but that he had been on vacation. His face was sunburned, except for the two circles around his eyes where he had been wearing sunglasses. That was so funny. Gardus came into the class and saw him, Sharon, the *'pretending sick'* student. Gardus said, *"I am almost blinded by your sunburnt face! So you have been sick, huh?"*

Sharon said, *"I'm sorry."*

"What?" said Gardus, *"I can't hear you."*

"I said, I'm sorry I lied."

"Sorry, I can't hear you," said Gardus. *"Your answer sounds like an old, frustrated woman from the geriatric department."*

Sharon said, *"I lied, and I'm sorry."*

"Yes, you did," said Gardus. *"Do you really mean that you are sorry? Okay. For tomorrow, you will be required to write an article on 'Why it is not good for me to lie.'"* For the next week, you will also stay on at school longer, when the adult students are here, and, by the way, I will also be calling your parents to report your lying.

I was astounded by Gardus's response to Sharon's lie. Other teachers might have laughed Sharon's stunt off. They may have said, *"This is no big deal. Kids will be kids."* But at the same time, I appreciated the actions Gardus took, because it is a big deal to lie. To let the lie slide, to not confront it, is actually to support the lie. Every lie needs to be responded to immediately. It must be cut from the root. Because each lie will be eventually discovered. It's bad enough to lie to yourself. That always hurts you, even if you can't see it at first. But lying to other people damages your connections to them and diminishes your ability to love and care for others.

The lies always, at some point, float on the water. Gardus wanted Sharon (and the rest of our class) to understand that lying is never the acceptable choice. He did this by showing us that the person who chooses to lie then has to face their lie. After that experience, I was filled with a determination to always be truthful. In this world of illusion, our honesty is a solid foundation for self-respect and for showing that we care and respect others.

The way that Gardus taught us was always through experience.

In sociology class, we learned about a crime ring. Gardus thought it would be good for us to visit a prison to learn about that environment. He arranged for this, and we gained some insight into prison life. It was a really powerful experience to meet murderers and other criminals, and see how the wrong choices could lead to misery, and even rob a person of the ability to make other choices. I could feel the drama in the prison atmosphere. I asked Gardus a lot of questions while we were there.

Gardus said to me, *"Talia, you have a deep curiosity about people. You should consider becoming a social worker."* Although

I ended up following a different path in life, I was touched by my teacher's insight, and in a way, he was right, because all my work has always been centered around helping people.

The other thing that was very important to Gardus was that we never took drugs. He and other wonderful teachers fostered a group of students and trained us to be leaders against drug abuse. The woman who guided us was the wonderful school counsellor, Noga. Perhaps the most powerful memory from this period of learning came from Gardus.

He said something like, *"If my son or a friend was a drug addict and he didn't want to get help, and he came to my door, I would shut the door in his face. Sometimes people need to sink to the 'juice of the garbage' to understand that they need help. You can't help someone that doesn't realise that they need help."* At the time he said that, it seemed harsh, but today, I clearly understand what he meant. He was absolutely right.

You cannot actually help anybody except yourself. And when you do that, you become an example: you help people by the way you allow yourself to be. In your power, you can live in peace with yourself and be a lighthouse for others.

If the person in front of you doesn't admit to himself that he needs help and doesn't take responsibility, the way I learned to deal with it is to love myself and take care of myself. On the other hand, if that person asks for my help, but doesn't throw his problems on me, which means he doesn't drain my energy, but agrees to do what he can and should to assist in his problem, then my heart and my hands will be always open to him for support.

Whatever he needs, but that's it. My job is finished. I will not carry his problems with me. I'm then back to focusing on myself.

But once someone asks for me to fix his sorrow and his problem, but won't step up and help work out his solutions, I can't help. Well, perhaps the best way for me to help someone with that attitude is to let him face the struggle of searching within himself until he acknowledges that he does have the power to overcome his problems, if he's willing to work change, and make better choices.

In our class, one of the students became chozer *B'tshuvah* which means in Judaism that a person embraces the religion, changes their lifestyle according to the religious requirements, and follows all of the rules that go with that. Another student became *chozer b'sh'eilah*, which means that a person leaves active religious Jewish practice and chooses to no longer follow that lifestyle. Inevitably, this created a lot of stress between them (they had never been friends, but they had been in the same class), especially in *Tenach* (Bible studies). The boy who became *chozer b'sh'eilah* was rejected by his own family. Gardus adopted him like a son. He would always say, *"You are free to choose. You can choose whatever your heart tells you to do. You have so much courage to make a move like this. I support you."*

In sociology class, we learned about the many different religious groups in Judaism. Gardus thought it would be beneficial for us to visit an extremely religious group, so he took us to Mea She'arim, *'The 100 Gates'*. This is one of the oldest Jewish neighbourhoods in Jerusalem, where members of an extremely conservative group live. When you visit this district, it feels as if you have travelled back in time a hundred years. Of course, the girls had to be modestly dressed, wearing long skirts and covering their arms. I remember walking down the street there and being spat in the face. Spitting three times and knocking on wood three times is a superstitious protection against negative energy and bad luck. I was told it was my good luck to be spat on. The girls and the boys of our class were separated when we arrived. The boys went to the Yeshiva, the Jewish institution that focuses on the study of traditional texts, mainly the Talmud and the Torah, and met with the Rabbi there.

We, the girls, went to a woman's house who helped girls in the process of *Chazara B'tshuvah* as they implemented the strict lifestyle and religious rules that this community required.

The women welcomed us to the house and fed us. While we were there, there were many arguments at the table. One of the students from my class was very opinionated and asked many questions. *"Why do you live like this? There is life outside this place! Why don't you serve in the army?"* She was so intense, she was almost shouting.

Some of my classmates were quiet, and others were loud, shouting as well. I felt conflicted through this situation. On the one hand, this woman had invited us to her house and shared her life with us in such generous hospitality. It didn't mean that we were allowed to come into her house and criticize the way she chose to live.

On the other hand, when you receive an invitation from a religious person, you sometimes sense that underneath all their generosity that they offer to you, their agenda is that you become more religious, which is also a big criticism of how we live.

But this was also fascinating, because it's a microscope on a problem that we deal with in Israel, which is how religious and unreligious people interact with each other.

I was shocked and surprised by the way they lived in Mea She'arim. There were so many Bibles, stacked from the floor to the ceiling and filling shelves from wall to wall, and there were so many children everywhere, but not a single toy. The separation between men and women was so extreme. When I saw men on the street, they lowered their heads and avoided eye contact. Even children as young as three were segregated from the other sex, in their play and in their schooling. I asked the woman who owned the house we visited what she would do if one of her eleven children decided to become *chozer b'sh'eilah*. She told me, *"I will not accept him as my son."* After that, I had no more questions.

I was shocked by her answer to me. I kept looking at her with wide eyes and an open mouth. I thought to myself, *"Oh my God, how can a person become so extreme about their religious beliefs without understanding the real meaning of it?"* Her words contradicted the true spirit of Judaism.

We have a well-known story in Judaism. Once a student came to his rabbi and asked, *"What is all about the essence of the Torah?"* The rabbi said, *"That you love someone as you love yourself."*

This is what I thought about that woman: By not accepting your own son by the way he may choose to live, you not only defy your religion, but you also don't take the challenge to learn through motherhood to love your child unconditionally.

Our hostess understood my feelings by the shocked look on my face. I couldn't understand why she didn't look inside for more meaning and truth. But it was not my responsibility to show her and teach her.

Gardus exposed us to politics and national customs. When there were elections in Israel, Gardus invited all of the candidates to come and speak at our school. All of the students from Ancory Rishon Lezion, and all the students from other Ancory-affiliated schools around the country came together in a big hall. One of the persons who spoke was Benjamin Netanyahu, who was later the Prime Minister of Israel.

We had a microphone in the corner of the room where we could ask questions. I was nervous and shaking, but I went to the corner and asked Benjamin Netanyahu, *"Why did you continue to talk to the crowd when people were screaming, 'Kill Yitzhak Rabin?' (the previous Prime Minister, who was later assassinated by an Israeli extremist). Why didn't you tell them to stop shouting 'Kill Rabin'?"*

Benjamin Netanyahu spoke for half an hour, and went around and around in circles, but never directly answered my question.

I stopped shaking after I asked my question, which was very direct, but even if I didn't get an answer, I was very relieved because my truth came out.

No matter how powerful the person in front of you is, no matter their talent for verbal expression, people will never forget your own words and actions, especially if you speak truthfully and sincerely, from your heart.

One thing I learned from this exposure to politics: I truly believe that for us to wisely choose a leader, we need to look at him, and not just listen.

We need to lower the volume on the remote control and look carefully at the body language, facial expression, and their audience's response.

How often does the candidate put his right hand on his heart, which means he is talking from his heart?

Or maybe one hand is in the pocket, all of the time – which means the words are only half the truth.

How often do his eyes look down – which means a lie.

Or maybe he looks towards the ceiling – which means, help me God.

Is the smile on the face full, which means generous? Or is it a half smile – which means disrespect?

And more important and interesting, how do people react to the person? Are they calm? Relaxed? Feeling brotherhood? Peaceful? Is there an atmosphere of enthusiasm? Or is there a sense of anger and hostility?

Verbal violence creates violent actions, and the characteristics of candidates can create chaos in society. Energy is who we really are, not our words.

Politicians know how to manipulate people through words. It seems that the people who have talent in talking are the people who choose to be ministers in the world. The world of illusion.

But this experience pushed me even more to say my truth, no matter who is standing in front of me.

Gardus was well known for being an unusual educator. Every year on Yom Hashoah (the Holocaust Memorial Day), we would have a formal ceremony. Gardus decided to present it in a different way. He invited the students to write a play, even a comedy, to express the feelings of the day. He received a lot of criticism about this, but he explained that it was more relevant, more touching, and meaningful than the formal, didactic way of remembering the holocaust.

I remember the play was very funny and modern, and different from anything else I'd seen in my life. But at the same time, it was very respectful, and it kept my focus. Almost like hearing the same song lyrics, but accompanied by a different tune.

In the same way, how dare he take a painful subject like that and make it funny! But ironically, it is the only play I've seen in my life that I remember well.

It doesn't matter how we say things, but how they make us wake up our feelings. And Gardus woke us up.

Every year, in the middle of the school year, we would have a parent-teacher meeting. I remember one of them very clearly. Gardus gave me a small present, a book full of funny stories. But it wasn't what he gave me; it was what he said to me that I remember so clearly. He said, *"I do understand your difficulty. You are very mature for your age. It is hard to be you."* I felt this was the first time in my life that someone saw me in my true colours. At that time in my life, I was really insecure and very shy. I didn't feel comfortable around people. I couldn't speak confidently in public, just one-on-one with friends. I never socialized in group settings. I hardly ever spoke at school. On the outside, I appeared to be very confident, but inside, I felt oversensitive, and I was very protective of myself. Gardus' words gave me comfort and helped me to understand my personal struggles with other students at school. I had always wanted to ask Gardus if he believed in me, but I never had the courage to ask. I guess this question isn't something you need to ask someone else. I needed to find my own belief in myself.

When we finished school, I wrote a letter to Gardus, just to say thank you, and we met for a coffee. I asked him what drove him. He was surprised. *"I've never been asked that question by a student before, only by teachers and parents. My belief in the worth and promise of each individual student is what drives me."*

When I joined the army, I had a few difficulties and went to see Gardus for advice. Gardus sat with me in his office and listened to my story. He encouraged me and gave me very good advice. Many years later, I wasn't surprised to find out that Gardus was still the director of Ancory. I guess when you are the Captain of *"Values"* and of *"Beliefs"*, you don't leave the ship for any reason.

I don't really think he understood how important he was to me. I had never seen someone like him before. His drive in life was to help and teach with an abundance of love, care, and devotion, and all to such a high level. It touched my heart to see him, being such a good person in a world of illusion. People like him are so extraordinary that I am moved to tears when I think about them. It was clear to me that he gave all that he could. I do believe that the most important job in society is to be an educator. That is what helps children to get onto the right track. If we had more teachers like Gardus, the face of society would change. Good teachers are like those who prepare the soil before planting a seed, creating an environment in which each student can grow to their full potential.

OUT OF THE BOX

My darling, my love, my sweet, sweet angel, in life, sometimes you will need to deal with problems. Let's change this word to challenges. Every challenge has a solution. If you can't find a solution, maybe you need to try something else.

If you use your courage once, you will use it more and more. If you use your creativity once, you will use it more and more. By the way, this works the opposite way, too.

Let me tell you a story about this.

When I was twenty-four, I was a support worker in a hostel for people with mental illnesses. I did this job for about three years. Most of the people in the hostel suffered from schizophrenia, but they also suffered from other conditions. Schizophrenia is a mental disorder often characterised by abnormal social behaviour and failure to recognise what is real. People with this type of disorder may hear voices or may believe that other people read their thoughts or plot to harm them. This can terrify people with the illness and make them withdrawn or extremely agitated.

The purpose of the hostel was to teach people the skills that would prepare them for independent life in the community. My role was to teach them how to cook and clean the house, to make sure they bathed themselves, to manage a budget for shopping, and of course, to provide support when they needed it. Most of the residents there had years of repeated breakdown events. Half of them worked in menial jobs for a few hours a day to keep themselves busy. They did small jobs in factories, for example, like putting plastic bags in boxes.

There were two social workers on the hostel staff whom the residents saw twice a week. There was a hostel manager and six support workers. Because of tight budgets, I was often alone with residents, without supervision or the support of the social workers. I worked three times a week from 3pm till 8am, with sole-charge and responsibility for ten people. You could always reach the manager or the social workers by phone if you needed to, but if any problem arose, I was the person responsible until such a time as backup arrived.

Most of the time, a social worker is in the hostel for a few hours and has private chats with the residents. Also, the manager was there. Once a week, we had a meeting to update and support each other in the work we were doing in the hostel.

A lot happened in the hostel, but I would like to tell you about one particular person. I will call him Shimon. Shimon was around forty years old. He was 160cm tall and overweight. The residents were on so much medication that most of them were overweight. His head was always tilted to the side, so that he often drooled out of the corner of his mouth. He wore a kippah and had the kindest blue eyes. I loved him a lot. He was a wonderful person, really kind to everyone and he always carried out his duties. Every day he worked for three hours in a factory. In the morning, he always prayed. He always greeted and welcomed everyone. Shimon was suffering from schizophrenia. When he became psychotic, it was very difficult to manage his care. Out of the blue, he would start to scream without stopping. He would run around with a knife in his hand, talking to the ghosts that had come to take him.

Unfortunately, these episodes would usually end with forced hospitalization and electric shock treatments. It is important for me to say to you, darling, that these people are not deliberately dangerous. Not at all. But for them, being in a psychotic state is like falling down a bottomless well. They are out of control. Everything that is on the inside breaks out and overwhelms them. At such times, they need help.

Shimon would often have psychotic episodes, and each time the same movie would play: he would be taken to hospital, be treated the same way, and eventually return drained and deflated to the hostel. Whenever he came back, he looked like a balloon that had lost all its air.

Once, after he had been hospitalized, I went to visit him. I saw him sitting in a chair in his pajamas. When he saw me, he jumped like a firework; he was so excited to see me. I excused myself quickly and told him, *"I'll be back in a minute, I have to go to the loo."* But actually, I needed to cry. It was so hard for me to be there. I felt so guilty. I was so tired and needed rest, but I could see what it meant to him for me to be there, and it broke my heart.

When I was back from the bathroom, Shimon took my hand and showed me to all the nurses, and all of the people there, introducing me to everyone.

"Look, this is Talia," he would say. *"She came to see me."* It was so poignant to watch his simple delight in my company. I felt such pure love for him in that moment. When Shimon returned to the hostel, he would usually be relaxed for a few days. Then the cycle would start all over again.

One day, when I arrived for my shift, Mayan, the other support worker, informed me that there was a problem. *"Taliush, Shimon has started again."*

"Yes, I can hear the screaming."

"If you need help, call me. But if it gets worse, call the hospital, okay? We will try to keep him here if we can. Good luck, my friend. I hope he won't be too hard on you." Mayan was such a wonderful, big-hearted person.

I sat in our office at the top of the building, but you could hear everything. Shimon was screaming at ghosts, louder and louder. I needed first of all to solve a problem on the second floor; apparently, a toilet was out of order. I called a plumber and asked him to come over. I told him to look for me, Talia, explaining that I was the supervisor on duty. Then, I decided to try something with Shimon, who was still screaming. I went to his door with the master key.

"Hey, Shimon, open the door. You hear me?"

"What? Who is it? Is it Talia, the motherfucker fucking everyone in the hostel?"

"Yes!" I screamed back through the door, as loudly as him. *"It's Talia, the motherfucker fucking everyone in the hostel!"*

Now it's important for me to say to you, my darling, when someone is in a psychotic state, he isn't aware of what he's saying. He's in an unconscious mental state. When you allow yourself to break down in front of another person like this, I see that as a compliment. Shimon knew that I loved him unconditionally.

I screamed, *"Are you going to let me in, or do I have to break the door down?"*

"Go away, bitch!"

"Okay, I'm going to break the door," I screamed. I unlocked the door, but kicked it open, so it made a loud bang. Shimon

was standing in the middle of the room with his arms in the air.

"Yes?" I screamed, hoping the neighbours wouldn't call the police. "What's the problem?"

"The ghosts, they've come to take me, bitch."

"Where, Shimon? Where are the ghosts? Show me."

"Here," said Shimon, and he pointed to the ceiling.

"Okay. Let's throw them away. Go away motherfuckers," I screamed. "Shout with me, Shimon." We stood together and screamed into the air like it was the end of the world. "Okay, where else? Show me."

Shimon pointed at the floor. We screamed, "Go away! Get lost! You are the motherfucker ghost! You need to go to hell!" After a few minutes, all of the hostel residents were crowded around Shimon's door. They started to laugh and point. "Look, Talia's gone mental," they said. Shimon and I continued to scream.

"Motherfucker ghosts have come to take me!"

"They will not get you. Where else are they?"

"In the bed," he said.

"Come on, we have work to do. Go away, Devils! Go back to where you came from."

In the meantime, the plumber arrived.

"Excuse me," he said, pushing his way past the residents. *"I'm looking for Talia."*

"Wait one second, Shimon," I told him. *"Don't stop fighting the ghosts."*

I said to the plumber, *"Hi, I'm Talia. Thank you for coming. I will take you to the toilet that's broken."*

"No, no," he said. *"I'm looking for Talia, the supervisor."*

"That's me. I'm just playing." He looked at me as if I were a ghost, and ran away. Shit, I thought. What am I going to do with the toilet now? I went back to Shimon. He hadn't stopped shouting. *"Where else, Shimon?"*

"On the shelf!"

"Let's throw them away, go to hell! Motherfucker ghosts!" I screamed at the shelf. *"Now, Shimon, let's go and flush them down the toilet. They will disappear for good and never come back."* We went to Shimon's bathroom.

"Are you ready? When I count to three, flush the water. Okay?" I screamed, *"One, two, three! Now, Shimon, flush!"* He almost broke the handle.

He went quiet. He went to his bed and sat down on the edge, his head leaning to the side.

I couldn't believe it. I said to myself, *"Talia, don't say anything. Just leave the room."* I left. I went to check on the other residents, and after five minutes, passed by his room. Shimon was still sitting on his bed quietly. He hadn't moved. I left again, returning every ten or twenty minutes, pretending that I had come to do something. All remained quiet. At ten o'clock, Shimon went to sleep. I stepped close to the bed and saw that he had really fallen asleep. I couldn't believe it. At midnight, I came by again to check on him. He was still asleep. It was unbelievable.

In the morning, Shimon came to see me before he left for work. *"Hi Talia, I've come to take my medicine."* It was as if nothing had happened.

"Great," I said. *"Have a wonderful day."*

Mayan arrived to swap shifts with me at 8am. *"How is Shimon?"* she asked me.

"He's great."

"What? How is that?" I told her everything.

It turned out that my approach actually helped reduce the frequency of Shimon's attacks. He still had them, but they happened less, and it was easier for people to help him when he had a serious episode.

My time in this job taught me so much, and I got a lot of satisfaction out of working with the residents at the hostel. I learned a lot about people with mental illness. I learned that people with mental illnesses are not dangerous. Actually, they are beautiful people who have to deal with many challenges.

I understood that people who suffer from mental illness are in a static, ongoing state. I was amazed at the richness of their inner life, and it made me deeply aware that all of us experience life according to our inner life, and not necessarily according to reality.

We react to the world through the lens of our inner life, and it makes me wonder sometimes. Maybe people who suffer from mental illness are more sensitive to the energy around them. From my experience, they don't have any ego.

The ego is often the filter that protects us, between what happens in our inner life and what affects us from the outer life.

The *'me'* and *'I'* of our ego is such an open door that everything can come in without any sense of who we are.

People with mental illness have big hearts and some sweet magic inside them. It was a pleasure and a blessing to work with them. They taught me to not judge by what I see on the surface. They filled my heart with compassion. From them, I learned to accept people as they are. I also learned that it is possible to love every person we meet, no matter what package they come in. These are lessons that have enhanced my life's journey, and I treasure them. I pass them on to you, in the hopes that you will also be amazed and touched by the people who come into your life.

SNEAK TO HEAVEN

In the night, when the angels come to kiss babies

before they sleep

Can you send me a rope to climb to heaven above?

I promise I will only come for a while

just to kiss your eyes

WHAT TO DO

My darling, my love, my only one, what to do in life is a big question, and it is a good question to ask. It's funny, now when I think about it, because there is not one single option, and not just one direction. If you really discover your own talent and follow it, you will also find great satisfaction. I guess we take life too seriously in our early age. The older we get, the more we understand that peace of mind is the most important thing. Everyone has unique and special talents, sometimes more than one. When we use our talents, we feel alive and satisfied because we are bringing something good to the world that also benefits and empowers us.

This experience also helps us develop our spirituality. When we use the gifts that we came to earth with, we feel as if we are on the right track. It's as if our soul understands what it was meant to do. But if we ignore our talents, if we don't use them, it's like a flower seed that has been denied water, good soil, and sunshine. It can't grow and show its beauty to the world. It will be stuck with its ability and potential locked inside, unable to reveal them.

There may come a time in your life when you feel like that stunted flower. If that ever happens, remember: It's never too late to change direction in life. It's difficult because it can be scary. Change may require a lot of consideration for issues such as financial security. And what if we don't succeed? That doesn't matter. The deepest regrets never come from failing; they come from not trying.

Because what does it mean to fail or to be successful? You may fail financially; your dream may not take flight as you wish, but you've gained something from this experience. You dare. And you felt that possibility, and the opportunity to change your reality. You expose yourself to different people, a different way.

So, you didn't make a lot of money, but you are more successful from your experience. And you learn to see yourself not through your situation, but by the light of your experience and by knowing who you are through outside evidence. You may meet people who do something that interests you. You may find your real calling by daring to change your life.

So you are never a failure; there is always some form of success.From the perspective of time, things look less intense and less dramatic. Not trying is like going around with a bag of stones on your back. You will always feel heavy.

It is never too late to do what your heart tells you. It is never too late to become happy; it is never too late to follow your passion. Most of the time, what is stopping you is fear, your own fear. Nobody is stopping you but you.

In order to make a course correction in our lives, we need to first ask ourselves: What is stopping me from doing what I want to do?

Take your time, my darling, and break it down. This fear that you face right now is not new. Another question that can help is to ask: What held me back in the past from doing things that I wanted to do? When you consider these questions, my darling, you set yourself free. After that, my love, write down the best scenario you can achieve if you follow your passion.

Now write the small steps that you can do today that will open the door to follow your passion. Like one drop of water dripping repeatedly over time creates an ornate stalagmite. Like a small stream over time carves out the mighty Grand Canyon. Rome wasn't built in a day, and your dream, your passion, won't spring full-grown overnight just because you know what you want. But if you take small, consistent steps, they will grow and grow until one day, you will be amazed that you have arrived at the summit of your dream.

At the same time, remind yourself that you are not alone, and have patience to wait and see how the cards fall. The universe will support you always.

Look for inspiration. Talk with people who dare to do what you want to do. Listen to them as often as you can, and if you feel people don't support your passion, move away.

Because not a lot of people follow their passion, and you want to be supported by people who dare. That is your true tribe. And in turn, you will also be someone who supports other dreamers and doers.

Ask yourself, my darling: What is my talent? What is inside me that can bring love to myself and to the world? Don't give priority to the job title or the amount of money. At the end of the day, what did you do that made you feel good? What did you give that made someone else feel good?

The happiest people I've ever met are the people who follow their own hearts. Unfortunately, it also seems that many people performing the most difficult and really important jobs do not get paid enough. Sometimes, they don't get paid at all. This is one of the strangest elements in this world of illusion. Why is the Truth contradicted in this way? Because in this world of illusion, the Truth is not always visible. Most of the time, we need to discover the Truth through our choices.

Thank God, we have amazing people here in the World of Illusion. Ask any five-year-old child what he will be when he grows up, and chances are, he already knows. He is close to his own nature. But as we grow up, the stress of society and the expectations of people close to us start to tighten and channel our options. It can disrupt our connection with our natural instincts. People want to be *'somebody'*. They seek fame and attention, fortune and power, when true happiness lies in being true to our hearts and dreams, in creating love and sharing love and accepting love. It is so easy to get confused in the world because society is so materialistic and competitive, but even so, we are all responsible for our own happiness, and true happiness comes from the heart, no matter what criticism we get.

Most of our day is spent in our workplace. We have to love what we do because otherwise, our days are a nightmare. When we do this, our job comes naturally for us, it brings us joy. So find your real job, according to your nature.

When I was a child, I was sure I was going to be a psychologist. I even started studying it, but even then I didn't have quiet in my heart. The question, *"What is my real talent?"* didn't leave me. Then, I had a vivid dream--one of those dreams that you sense is more than just a random collection of synaptic brain activity. In my dream, an old man came to me and told me that I should drop everything I was doing and become an alternative therapist by touch.

I followed my dream, and now I am working as an alternative therapist with massage, shiatsu, and reflexology. Actually, I have my own technique. I have an amazing treatment room where I see clients. My business is called **Bright Touch**. So many people have been under my hands during the years. Perhaps I will be the first person who dies from having massage oil in my blood vessels. This career choice has been the absolute perfect fit for me. It enables me to express love and to help people. I grew up because of it. I can feel energy going through my hands, recognise tension, detect *"blocks,"* and feel pain slowly disappearing under my fingers.

The natural wisdom of the body is unbelievable. I will tell you a few secrets here: every thought, belief, fear, any emotion you have about yourself, about others, and about the world, especially when you are attached to these feelings, every such thought changes the energy in your body. By your own thoughts, you create and alter your physical situation. When energy changes according to negative beliefs, you start to lose energy.

Every body part, or organ, functions according to your beliefs and thoughts. There are diseases that help you to be able to separate your soul from your body, to let go when it is time to pass away. This is a gift from the universe, one to be respected. The other diseases are also gifts.

In Hebrew, we call disease, *'Machalah,'* which means *'forgiveness from God'*. For healing, we say, *'Hachlamah'*, which means *'start from God'*. It's not shameful to have diseases. Don't blame yourself. To have disease or pain is a gift to get rid of something that doesn't belong to you. Something that blocks you from being who you are: an *'Explosion of Love'*.

To release negative beliefs, you need a great deal of honesty, and you must consciously take responsibility to face the truth about yourself. Or, you can experience freedom through your body in ways that help you to relax your mind. Then you can feel the love in your body, and even in your soul.

That's what I'm doing. When people come to see me, I don't waste time; I do more than a hundred movements very fast, connecting with more than eighty pressure points. I create chaos of energy in the body. I fight with the mind of the person in order to relax their body, which helps their mind to relax. A person can then feel their own soul more. They can discover their original self. This brings people to where they are in the right place inside themselves, and healing starts to work. I don't need them to say to me they feel alive again. I look at their eyes shining with renewed energy and vitality, and I know I did a good job.

Touch is the strongest, universal language in the whole world. That's what I learned through my job: how you can affect and change the way people feel through touch.

Everyone gives the best when they follow their heart, not only for others but for themselves. To take action through love is to follow your heart, and you take care of yourself because you are following your passion. It's never too late to start doing what brings you joy; what is inside you that will bring you happiness. And by doing this, my darling, you cannot make a mistake. You already have everything do to this inside of you, but you need to give it freedom to take flight. It's like already owning a car, but to make it move, you need to push down the pedal. (So push, darling, push!)

Whatever you follow, follow your heart. I'm sure you have wonderful things to bring to the world. Whatever you do, I'm sure you will choose to do it for yourself. Don't forget, you are an *'Explosion of Love.'*

FUN

My darling, my love, my beautiful angel, you are an *'Explosion of Love,'* and part of agreeing to be who you are is to enjoy life. Enjoy the moment! There is so much fun and excitement in life. So much. The belief that we came here to suffer is wrong. We came to experience the beauty of life. To have fun is not about connecting with money or time but about connecting with a state of mind.

When we are in the right frame of mind, everything is fun. Wake up in the morning and be alive. Have a shower, eat, go for a walk, look at all of the trees standing proud, unashamed to be who they are. Go to the beach and look at the infinity of the ocean. Look at the sun, how she goes to sleep each night but never tires from rising again. What discipline nature has! What about us? We say, *'I don't wanna'*, *'I can't be bothered'*, *'I'm tired'*. What would happen if the sun said that? She's taking the day off or moving out with another planet, what then?

Listen to music, it will change your mood immediately. Spend time with people who have the same courage as you, to become human beings. If I want to get to know someone quickly, I ask them, *"What do you do for fun?"* Unfortunately, sometimes people need to think about it. Enjoy every moment, my darling. In Hebrew, when we make a toast, we say *l'chaim*, which means *'to life'*. Tonight I make a toast to you: *"L'chaim, my love, for your life."*

Let me tell you a story about the fun I've had in life.

I learned to ride a bicycle when I was twenty-seven years old. Here's how that happened.

At the age of twenty, I decided I wanted to learn to ride. I asked my parents, *"Why didn't you teach me before?"*

"We wanted to," they said. *"But you didn't. We decided not to fight with you about it. We respect your opinion."*

"Okay, but now I want to learn."

"You are twenty years old, Talia. Good luck to you."

Over the next several years, many people tried to teach me to ride a bicycle, but without success. Every lesson always ended with a big argument and disappointment.

Every lesson always seemed to go like this:

"Okay, so sit on the seat and pedal. I will hold your seat from the back. I will not leave you," they would say.

"Aha, but if you weren't going to leave me, why would you say that? It only means that you are going to leave me."

"No, no," they would say. *"I didn't mean it like that."*

"What do you mean, 'no, no'? If you said it, you're going to leave me, so why did you even mention it? Now I don't trust you."

And of course, they always left me.

One day, at around twenty-one years old, I crashed and found myself in a huge garbage bin. Children and parents stopped to stare at me. The parents told their children, *"You see why you need to learn now?"* The children peddled away so fast, looking at me in shock while I climbed out of the garbage bin.

Time passed. I found myself walking along the street in Tel Aviv one evening. I noticed so many people riding on bicycles, and I thought to myself, it looks like such fun! I wanted to ride, too. Then suddenly I knew who would teach me to ride, once and for all; it was my friend, Marin. She was the one. Marin is an amazing woman. She has lots of children, and she also runs a children's day-care. She must be rich with patience. I called Marin.

"Yes, sure," she said. *"I can teach you."*

"But," I said. *"I don't like that thing where you hold onto my seat and then leave me."*

"Talia, I won't touch you with a single finger. Come tomorrow afternoon."

The next day at Marin's house, she showed me her ten-year-old son's bicycle. *"You're going to learn on this,"* she said. We went to the park with all her children. There were lots of other children there, too.

Marin lowered the seat of the bicycle as far down as it would go. I sat on the seat with my legs on the ground.

"Great, Talia. Now just hold the handlebars and walk forward with your feet on the ground. Feel comfortable on the bike. When you are ready, lift your legs into the air. If you don't feel comfortable, put your legs back on the ground. Great! You're doing great! You see how easy it is?

Now, when your legs are in the air, put them on the pedals and start to pedal. If you feel insecure, put your legs back on the ground."

I walked forward with the bicycle. Then I put my legs in the air as she had instructed. Then I put my feet on the pedals and pedalled and pedalled.

Marin shouted, *"TAAAALIAAAAAAA!!!!! You're riding a bicycle!!!!!!"*

Behind me, all of Marin's children and all of the children in the park followed me as I rode.

I was riding a bicycle! By myself!

Whooooooaaa!!

"What now?" I yelped. *"How do I stop?"*

"Put your legs on the ground again!" she said. What a feeling.

"Oh my God," Marin said. *"It only took you twenty minutes to learn."*

"I can't wait to finish the Tour de France," I said.

It was so much fun riding a bicycle that I wanted to buy one for myself. I went to a shop and said I wanted to buy the best bike they had.

"You see this bicycle," the shop guy said. *"It's like a BMW. The seat is full of special gel, so even if you ride all day, you won't be sore. The frame is made of aluminium, so it's light."*

"Mmm, I'll take it," I said. I had never spent so much money in my life. But this is my first bicycle. Of course, I bought all the professional bicycle riding gear. People were proud of their property and cars. Me? I was proud of my BMW-quality bicycle and my complete collection of Russian literature.

One afternoon, a client came to see me at home. We had a conversation about the wacky people we had seen. He told me about a hilarious sight he had seen on the street. *"Listen to this, Talia. This morning, when I was sitting in traffic, I saw this ridiculous woman completely dressed in professional riding gear, struggling to sit on her bicycle."*

"Tell me, please, did this ridiculous woman have a blue top on and a red helmet, and was she wearing black sunglasses?"

"Yes," he said. *"How did you know that?"*

"Well, my friend, that ridiculous woman was me."

"Oh, Talia, I'm so sorry," he couldn't stop himself from laughing. *"But why were you dressed like that if you don't know how to ride?"*

"First of all, I do know. Secondly, it's a new bicycle, and I was getting comfortable with it, okay?"

And I did feel comfortable on it. I rode everywhere on it, all the time. I rode to the beach, to the park, to my friends, and on busy roads.

"Hey, Talia!" a friend called out to me one day when I was cycling on the road.

"Hey," I called back. *"I can't stop now, sorry."*

Whenever I heard that an adult didn't know how to ride a bike, I would call them immediately. *"I have something important to tell you,"* I would say. *"Don't live life without knowing how to ride."*

"Thank you very much for your advice, Talia," they would say.

Every person I met would know about it.

"Hi, Talia! How are you?"

"Good," I would say. *"I know how to ride a bicycle."*

"What — just now?"

"Yes, just now."

I even wrote an article about learning to ride.

The same thing happened to me when I learned to play the piano. My friend left her piano at my house because she didn't have room for it in hers. Every day, I would wake up and look at this piano. One morning, I sat up in my bed like the waking dead. I woke up with only one thought in my head: I am going to play this piano.

I practiced for hours every day. My teacher thought I was very talented, but the truth is, I drove everyone around me crazy. I couldn't stop. After a year, I was able to play Beethoven's Moonlight Sonata. It made me feel so happy and proud of myself, so full of joy to be able to play that. It made me understand that everything is possible. Who said that to be able to play the piano, you have to be young? I want you to understand that if you're driven by passion and joy, and you're having fun, the sky is the limit. As long as you're enjoying the process, the goal doesn't exist – just passion and joy.

In life, we have unlimited options for expressing our joy. Never lose curiosity in life, my darling, l'chaim, for your life to be.

A RUMOUR FROM HEAVEN

I heard rumours from heaven above

said the tree to the earth,

that very soon we'll have a special visitor.

So, I will put on the best leaves I can grow.

I will water my soil, said Earth.

Rumours are running from heaven to earth,

that soon an abundance of love

will come swimming here, said the ocean to the fish.

So I will clean my deepest water.

I will shine my scales, said the fish.

There are rumours from heaven,

said the moon to the sun.

That soon we will have a special visitor on eEarth.

So, I will open my arms and send a lot of warmth,

said the sun.

I will turn on the army of stars in the night,

said the moon.

A rumour is running from heaven to earth,

said my soul to my mind. That soon, an

abundance of love will visit me.

So I will start to pray.

CONNECTION

My darling, my sweet love, one of the amazing things we experience in this life is the connection between people. It's hard to explain it because it's a feeling, and it happens like magic. You meet someone, and you feel immediately connected to him. You feel an *'Explosion of Love'*. You feel he speaks your *'innerlife's'* language. You feel as if you have known each other for at least a thousand years. He can see your true colours immediately. You have never met before, you don't have the same blood, but you feel like he is your own brother. You feel blessed and loved. He feels like *'home.'*

I don't know what this is. We sometimes use the word *'soul-mates.'* Maybe that is a good description: Two people who meet at the same level of their souls? Maybe we come from the same place in the *'other world'*? Maybe we have the same element in our souls, or we have come here for the same mission? Whatever it is, it's a Blessing.

Time loses meaning because your feeling is not based on the past or time; it is based on connection. Which is strong evidence for us, that in life, we have more going on than we can see. Something that is bigger than us, that magnetizes people and draws them together. At times like that, you will sense that the feeling of closeness and connection and familiarity is really coming from another world.

And how we recognize them is by the familiar smell of their fart...?

No, seriously, the beautiful love feeling in the heart, and this strong feeling we feel when we look in their eyes.

It feels like it's meant to be. It was written in the book of life before you even met. If people don't believe in God, and in other life, how can they explain this situation? The meeting of our soul-mate – someone who we feel we knew a long, long time ago.

It is the connection directly from Divine (or *'de wine'*), and it always happens at the right time, in the right situation, during our life.

Now we get a sense of what it is all about, and how we should feel in our heart. We need to feel love, and we get a reminder of this by meeting our soul mate. If we are lucky enough, or if we are supposed to share life with our soul mate, we've actually found heaven on Earth. But it is not always a romantic connection; sometimes it is simply a reminder that love is the essence of the universe. Either way, when this happens, we are blessed.

There have been times when I travelled extensively, and I experienced this feeling with a lot of people, which continues to the present. When we travelled and then went our separate ways, we would always say, *"I will see you in 5 minutes."* Which meant, *"I don't know when I'm going to see you next, but I know what I will feel when I see you. It will feel like I saw you five minutes ago."*

Connection is something that happens beyond our control. It's not in our hands. I was quite worried when I went back to visit Israel after being away for so long. My brother had five children, and my sister had two children. Six of them had never met me before. I thought to myself, *"Dear me! I went so far away for so long. I'm such a crazy woman!"* One of my best friends said to me, *"Talia, you went so far away. If you had gone just a little farther, you'd have fallen off the planet."*

I thought to myself, *"These children don't know me. I'm a total stranger to them. What am I doing?"* But I couldn't resist my inner voice that had guided me to New Zealand. My visit in Israel surprised me and showed me once again what connection means. The first time I met my nephews and my nieces, a wave of love washed over us. It was an unbelievable ***'Explosion of Love'***. You can never hurt anybody if you are guided by your inner voice.

And connection is without time, place, or limits. Totally blessed.

LOVE

My darling, my beautiful love, one of my friends, one week before he passed away said to me, *"Hey Talia, you know I'm nearly finished. I feel I'm going to pass away very soon. I know now what life is about."*

"Tell me, please. What is it?"

"It's love. Everything, everything, everything is LOVE."

NEW ZEALAND

My darling, my love, my only one, I present to you: New Zealand! .... Or according to the Māori people, the first settlers of New Zealand, Aotearoa *"The Land of the Long White Cloud."* I wonder now, are you going to be born here? I guess if I'm still here . . . but who knows? I have learned in life, *"never say never"* because *"never"* has a way of becoming reality. It's almost as if the universe will test you on it.

Abracadabra, from Aramaic, means, *"I create as I speak."* Wherever you are going to be born, here or somewhere else, be sure I will show you New Zealand. Oooh yeah!

When I first came here six years ago, I couldn't understand this country; it was so quiet, so relaxed, so beautiful. I almost thought New Zealand lied to me. Come on, show me your real face! But as I travelled with friends by van on the South Island, I came to understand that this is not fake, this really is the true New Zealand. It's a relaxing, beautiful, and quiet place. Oh my God! Can life really be like this?

If we imagined every country as the equivalent of a body's organs, then Israel would be the digestive system of the world, but New Zealand would definitely be the feet of the world. There is something here that makes you feel very close to nature. Something in the air, the energy of this country is on a high spiritual level. Actually, the highest I have ever experienced. The beauty of nature is perfect. The trees, the flowers, the mountains, the lakes... ooooh the lakes are unbelievable. The ocean. It is almost as if God has taken a paintbrush and painted a painting. It is almost as if when God was creating the beauty of nature, he thought about New Zealand. There are places here that feel and look untouched by humans. Pure beauty. It takes your breath away. There are no snakes or foxes here.

After my first visit to New Zealand, I started working on a cruise ship and travelled to twenty-six other destinations around the world, but in every other place that I went to, I would say the same thing: yes, it is beautiful, but I've been in New Zealand and haven't seen anywhere more beautiful yet.

It's like the tree isn't ashamed to be a tree. The flower is proud to be a flower, as if they are primping and preening all the time. Here nature shows off her colours. The green is the best green I have ever seen. Red is truly red. Blue is the most intense blue ever. The element here is that as you surrender into all the beauty of nature and breathe deeply, that it opens your heart.

Trees here grow to be really big because of an abundance of rain. Trees can open their arms to the sky and grow long branches. The same thing happens to your heart. You can open your heart and grow as much as you can. Sometimes I get the feeling that New Zealand isn't part of the real world, but rather sort of an in-between place, like the entrance to a fairytale world. There is this world, and the other world, and New Zealand in the middle. New Zealand is like a baby in the womb waiting to be born, surrounded by oceans.

For me, New Zealand is the gate to the world. Good things come first to New Zealand, then spread to the world. It is not by mistake that New Zealand was the first place in the world where women were able to vote. Many good things have started here. New Zealand is an immigrant country, especially Auckland, where I live. When I came here, I caught the bus to run my errands. There was an Indian driver, and a Japanese girl near me. I went to the bank, and the man who served me was Serbian. I went to the Post Office, and the woman there was Dutch. Oh, I like it here so much. Here, people don't care where you are from. Everyone is on the same level. Everyone reacts to you according to your personality.

I have met so many Arabic Muslim people here and had many conversations with them. In Israel, I never got the chance to meet many Muslims because of the difficulties that we face there. But here in New Zealand, it is possible. It is such a shame that extremists create so much chaos and stress that people caught in between are unable to connect with each other. In New Zealand, I can understand that Jewish and Muslim people are actually very close by nature. We should live like brothers and sisters, with love and acceptance of each other's ways. I hope one day that those caught between the extremists will be able to take control. Then we will have an opportunity to accept each other and have a chance to really meet from the heart, not from the past.

One friend of mine who used to live in New Zealand and later lived in many other countries around the world eventually returned to New Zealand. I asked him, *"So, why New Zealand? What is New Zealand for you?"*

He said, *"New Zealand for me is the place where I become who I am."*

I think it is the same for me.

New Zealand is full of secrets and puzzles. It looks and feels like an easy place to live, but when you tune out the noise of the ship's engines, you can hear the sound of the waves more clearly. In an environment where there is so much space and where you are isolated, you are able to hear your inner voice more clearly. This seems to be what happens here. In my whole life, I have never heard about or met so many people who have known those who have committed or attempted suicide. In my experience, New Zealand is a catalyst of the heart. It's a therapeutic place to clean the heart.

The first settlers here were the Māori people with chocolate brown eyes. Wise eyes, as rich as soil. When I look at them I feel that they are very close to the land. They are very grounded. They really know something about life. They have been here on many times before. For me, they look like very old souls. The culture is very rich, I love it, that they pray for nature. I think that's why New Zealand is so beautiful. Prayer is the highest form of energy that lifts and blesses. Nature illustrates this here. I love the respect given to ancestors. When a Māori person introduces himself, he presents all his ancestors and from where they arrived.

The majority of the people here are very nice and kind. (But like every place in the world, there are also a few idiots.)

We never know where our journey will take us; life is bigger than we think. Even though we don't always feel it, the possibilities are always there. Even if we don't see it, the possibilities are there, open for us. And each country has a unique element that can offer to us something we may need to receive and experience.

The options in the world are unlimited, and each place asks us to meet a different element in our inner life. Every country is blessed. Every country that makes you feel closer to your own self is the right place to be. You can't stay even one week more if it's not right for you. It's a very strong feeling... an unmistakable feeling. Just as the location of the stars in the universe is not a mistake, the location of people around the world is not a mistake.

Trust that the universe will lead you to your perfect place in the world. But won't it be so fun if you turn out, like me, to be a true child of New Zealand?

JOURNEY

I'm walking in the cave

I hold a candle in my hands

I move spider webs

I jump

into the ocean of hope

I swim with the sharks

I see a hill, and I climb on her.

At the top, I can see the sunset

dip into the clouds

Now, there is quiet serenity in my heart

And here you are

my abundance of love

surf in the rainbow above

TOP MEETING

My darling, my love, my only one, I'm going to tell you a story. Please follow the characters....

Once upon a time, when I was traveling in Russia, it was a dark night, the weather was freezing, and I was headed back to my hotel in Moscow, but I got lost. I couldn't find the hotel. It was so quiet on the street, as if everyone had decided to go to sleep at the same time. It was nearly midnight. As I wandered the dark streets, I passed a circular wooden door that was open just a little bit. I couldn't ignore the feeling that moved through me--a feeling of love and harmony.

I felt compelled to take a chance and see what was happening inside. I pushed open the door and found myself in a warmly lit tavern. A few people conversed at a bar. A large, circular table in the middle of the room caught my attention. Four men were seated, laughing and playing a game together. At a glance, I could see the fun they were having and the love that was between them. I noticed that there was a spare chair at the table. I came closer to them and asked, *"May I join you?"*

All of them stopped their game, looked at me, and smiled. *"Of course you can,"* they said. *"Everyone is welcome here."*

Now I noticed not just the love and the fun that they shared together. There were also four very handsome, very good-looking men. All of them.

"Hi," said the first man in the chair on the right. *"My name is Bob."* Bob had big blue eyes and long brown hair. His facial features were so gentle and radiant. He clearly had a good and giving heart.

"Nice to meet you," the second man introduced himself. *"I am Dror."* He was the oldest one there. He had long, curly, grey hair, dark blue eyes, and lots of wrinkles. He had full lips and a big, thick, white beard. He looked like someone you could count on. He knew the road. He had lots of experience and an aura of dignity.

The third one was Mustafa. He was wearing a white hat. He had olive skin and brown eyes. He had a small black beard, and he looked like a trustworthy man, someone loyal to his own truth, with an amazing ability to show love.

The last one who introduced himself was Lori. He was big, rotund, and bald. His facial features were in perfect harmony. He looked like he was almost falling asleep, but at the same time, he was very present in the moment. He looked like a generous man, willing to help everyone.

Bob said to me, *"Drink something. Hey, waiter, give our guest a Bloody Mary. Dror, what would you like to drink? The same?"*

"No, no," said Dror. *"Not this bloody drink again. I would like a beer. Thanks, mate. And for Mustafa and Lori, bring some soft drinks. They never drink alcohol."*

"Really," I said. *"Why not?"*

Mustafa looked at me with his good brown eyes. *"The reason I never drink alcohol is because I keep myself a hundred percent conscious. I never let myself lose control."*

Now Lori looked at me with his harmonious face and said, *"I don't drink alcohol because it's important to me to keep my feelings quiet. When you are under the influence of alcohol, your feelings become extreme."*

Dror, the oldest in the group, looked at him and said, *"I do agree with both of you, my dear friends. But sometimes it's good to lose control. Just to have a look at what is there under the surface. When you drink wine, your secrets come out."*

Bob started to laugh, *"Oh yeah, tell me about it! I remember me sitting with my twelve mates drinking red wine in our last dinner together. After the alcohol started to work, I understood that one of my mates had betrayed me."*

"*Well, we all have a different view, but we all accept each other. Cheers!*" said Dror, and everyone raised their drinks in a toast. "*For friendship forever.*"

"*Mmm,*" I said. "*What are you playing? I've never seen this game before.*"

"*Aha,*" said Dror. "*This game is called Union. You throw the dice, and then you count round the seats with the total number of your score. Then we ask this person a question. We are looking for similarity of opinion. It's good fun because we understand we are the same. Here, it's Mustafa's turn. Mustafa, throw the dice.*"

Mustafa got 1 and 4. "*Let's see,*" said Mustafa. "*If Bob is number one, and Dror is two, and I am three, and Lori is four, then number five will be you, Talia. So our first question to you is, What do you do?*"

"*Me? I am a traveller.*"

The four men started to laugh like it was the end of the world.

"*Aha,*" said Lori. "*We are also travellers. But Talia,*" said Lori, and a harmonious smile spread on his face. "*That's the story you tell to yourself. The only way you can travel is inside yourself. The outside isn't real. It just helps to reach down into your own truth. Sometimes we need a simplified metaphor to help us contemplate our own deepest consciousness.*"

"Beautiful," said Mustafa. *"I agree with you. I travelled a lot from an early age because I was an orphan. My parents died very soon after I was born, and I was raised by my uncle. After I grew up, I met my best friend Gabi, and he took me around the world. I can say to you that in every place that you visit, you have something to gain for your personality."*

"I agree with you, my friend," said Dror, and he scratched his white beard. *"I have also travelled for a long time because I felt I was being guided to some peaceful place where I could get straight to God. Sometimes you test your own truth by your own patience."*

"I am totally with you," said Bob, and he put his hand on the right shoulder of Dror.

"Hey, Bob," said Dror. *"You have such an amazing touch."*

"Dror," said Bob. *"I have to say to you that I travelled to the same places that you did. In every place that I've been to, I had so much work to do. Every moment is precious. But I'm not complaining. You see, I'm always happy to give everything I have, even if people are not wanting to listen."*

"Great," said Mustafa. *"Now we finish this circle. Put your hands in the middle of the table. You too, Talia."*

"Union! Forever!" all the men shouted.

"Okay, your turn," Lori said to Bob. *"Throw the dice."*

"Ooh la la", said Lori. *"Number 6 and 6. It reminds me of* someone's phone number. *Another 6 and he'll be here faster than you can think. Six and six is twelve. Starting from Lori, the round lands on you again, Talia."*

"So," said Bob. *"The question for you is: what is your fear?"*

"Mmm," I said. *"I guess my fear is that I will live my life alone."*

"Thank you for your honesty," said Bob. *"Let me tell you something about fear. The biggest fear I had was when I was alone in my biggest crisis. Everyone twisted my truth. I thought nobody understood me. Nobody accepted my truth, but I was willing to die for my truth. Afterwards, I saw that Truth is stronger than fear as long as you remain loyal to yourself. Ask Dror, he almost killed his own son because of fear."*

"Seriously, Dror?" I said. *"You really tried to kill your own son?"*

"Let me explain it to you, Talia. My biggest fear was that I might cheat on myself. Cheating on my Truth. After such a long time of waiting for a son, my wife Shoshana and I finally had one. I felt that I didn't deserve him. I couldn't believe this blessing. So I tried to kill this fear. But I didn't really intend to kill my son. It was an attempt to kill my fear."

"Ohh," I said. *"Thank you for your honesty."*

"Actually, Talia, honesty attracts honesty."

"I guess it's my turn," said Mustafa. *"My fear was that I was a stupid man. Because of the circumstances of my childhood, I didn't get an education. I actually don't know how to read or write, so I thought I had nothing to offer. But my friend, Gabi, thought differently. He often came to visit me, and he believed in me. It took me a long time to accept that even I had a lot to offer, and that I had lots of inner knowledge. Once I understood that it was best not to draw attention to my fear, then all my wisdom was able to come out. Gabi helped me with my writing."*

Lori smiled. *"Beautiful, my friends. I also have a fear to share with you. My own fear is to be stuck and not to move on in life. So to deal with my fear, I took it to the maximum. I didn't do anything. I just sat quietly and waited. I agreed to be nothing. Then one day I heard my inner voice inside me, and then I understood that when you surrender to your situation, then you can sink and become immersed into your inner truth."*

"Wow, amazing. You are all actually thinking the same way, but each of you explains it differently."

"Yes, Talia," Lori smiled to me with his harmonious face. *"We all dealt with our fears. We each allowed them to unfold until there was space for the truth to come out."*

"Actually, my dearest friend," said Dror. *"Your biggest fear is sitting on your biggest secret."*

"Let me add something here," said Mustafa. *"Our lives show that we all transfer our fear to the opposite side. We all use and*

observe our fears to show us our weaknesses. In this way, knowledge of our fears leads us to the discovery of our strengths. Fear is the opposite of strength, like the two sides of the same coin. Your fear is the reflection of your strength, and once you break free from your fears, you will receive your true secret, your power."

"Absolutely right," said Bob, and he finished his glass of Bloody Mary.

"Let me help you here, Talia. If your biggest fear is to be alone, your secret is that you are a people person. That is your strength. Your mission in life."

"Come on, mates!" Said Lori. *"Hands in the middle – Union!'*

"Okay, my turn," said Mustafa, and he threw the dice. *"Two and One. Let's see. I will start with me, I'm number one, two is Lori, and three is you again, Talia!"*

"Funny." They all started to laugh. *"It's always you,"* said Bob.

"Not by mistake," said Dror. *"Everything that happens has a reason. Now we will change the rules of the game. You may ask us the questions. You probably have lots of questions."*

"Aha," said Mustafa, and he winked with his right eye.

Lori looked at me with his harmonious smile. *"Be careful what you ask for,"* he said. *"Because you are going to get it."*

"Okay, so I would love to hear your answer to my question: what is the real problem in the world?"

All the men started to laugh so much. Mustafa started choking from laughter. Dror patted him on the back and asked if he needed a glass of water.

"No, I'm okay. It's just so funny!"

"What's so funny?" I asked.

Dror looked at me with his big smile. *"Talia,"* he said. *"Who says there's a problem?"*

"Come on," said Bob. *"Give her some explanation, she's curious. You are the oldest one, you can start."*

"Thank you, Bob," said Dror. *"But you will start first. Let's follow the seats at the table."*

Bob put his hands on top of my right hand as it rested on the table. Immediately, I felt a zing of energy go all around my body. Bob looked at me with his comforting look and moved his hands from mine. He left me with a relaxed feeling.

"Talia," said Bob. *"Here is my answer to your question: I was a tour guide, and I was a very famous one. I knew how to show people where to look to see beauty. One time, I said to my travel group, 'If you are travelling with me, I know the way.' But listen*

to this: people can take one statement and twist it according to their own interpretation or advantage.

After a while, a rumour was going round that I was the only tour guide that knew the way. People started telling stories about me that I was the best tour guide and that everyone should book trips just with me. But that's not what I was saying! Here at this very table are all of my best mates. They are also tour guides. They also know the routes very well. All my mates specialize in showing people the way. They may take a different road, but the destination is the same."

"That's beautiful," said Mustafa. "You are so humble. Talia, do you know that Bob was the biggest healer in the entire world?"

"Oh yes," said Dror. "With one hand, he could cure every disease."

"That is also a rumour," said Bob. "Let me explain it to you. When people came to see me with their diseases, I put my hands on their foreheads, the place between your eyebrows, and blessed them. I helped them to leave the situation that wasn't real for them. They cured themselves. Ask Lori--he knows how to explain that better than me."

"Thank you, my friend," said Lori. "I'm not sure if I can explain it better, but I can explain it differently. Well, between your eyebrows, there is a center that is sometimes called the third eye, or chakra number six. It presents the meeting between your physicality and your spirituality. When you relax physical

thought, you can connect to your spirituality. From there, you can empower yourself. If you are in the present, it is a present."

"Wow," I said. "So, I'm back to you, Bob. So, can you tell me, *what is the real problem in the world?"*

"The real problem in the world," said Bob, *"is that people twist the truth!"*

"Mmmm, interesting," I said. *"And what do you think, Dror?"*

Dror started to laugh. *"I'm not thinking. I already agree with my friend Bob. But let me explain this to you in a different way. Do you remember before, when we were talking about fear? When you fall into your own fears, and you don't take the time to face them, they start to control and trap you. All your actions start to become a way to avoid them. At that point, all of your actions are diversions from what is really important. When you are far away from who you really are, you only see the negativity around you. You think negatively, and your actions are negative. You cheat on yourself. You are not who you are meant to be. You are twisting the truth about yourself. Mustafa, my dearest friend, can explain it better than me."*

"I'm not sure about that," said Mustafa. *"You are a very wise man."*

"And you are a trustworthy one." And they hugged each other.

Mustafa then said, *"I agree with my dearest friend, but I will explain it to you in a different way... Talia, when you meet someone, you can easily see their weaknesses and their negative characteristics. Everyone can. But that is the easy part, because everyone also has positive characteristics as well. For example, if I showed you a beautiful but incomplete painting, you will only notice the missing colour in the bottom corner of the picture. Who cares about that? Unfortunately, that is all you will remember, and you will miss the beauty of the picture. If you don't use positivity in your actions towards yourself, your negativity will take control of you.*

Some time ago, I wrote a book about love, and the most hurtful thing for me is that people have taken my book about love and kill others in the name of this book. This is their own negativity. They can't see the beauty and the love in it because they are controlled by their own negativity, and when they use my book of love to cover that up, they are twisting the truth!"

"I totally agree with you, my dearest friend," said Lori. *"How people use your book also hurts me."*

From across the table, Dror and Bob stood up and said, *"Mustafa, we are all hurting from what people have done with your book of love."* Leaving their places, they rushed to hug Mustafa as he wiped the tears from his eyes.

"Talia," said Lori. "Do you remember when you asked the question, 'What is the real problem in the world?' and we started laughing? Do you know the reason we laughed so much?"

"No, I don't know the reason. Tell me, please."

"The reason we laughed so much is because problems don't really exist in the world. The problem is that people create problems because of the attention they give to negativity. For example, if I came to fight with you and you laughed and went away, there would not be a fight. People put attention on negativity and then make things bigger; and make them real. If people could develop a greater sense of peace inside themselves, they would not go looking for a fight, because the image of the fight would not exist inside them."

"Hands together in the middle of the table," said Bob. "Union!"

"I love you, all of you," said Bob.

"We love you, too!"

"Yes, I feel so flattered to sit with you," said Mustafa.

"What are you saying? I love all of you like my children."

"I feel the same," said Lori. "You are such an amazing man."

"What about me?" I said. "Do you love me also?"

"Stupid Talia," said Dror. *"Of course we do. Now we will not throw the dice because we know what we are going to get. So, Talia, what is your question?"*

"What is true love between a man and a woman?"

"Haha." Mustafa started to laugh. *"You hit the bull's-eye. But be careful of your ego so that your confidence doesn't go to your head. The most important thing is to be humble. Never claim to speak the truth. That is for other people to say about you."*

Bob said, *"As for your question, I think you need to ask Dror. He has had a lot of experience, and he has so many children."*

"Really," I said. *"How many, Dror?"*

"I have as many children as the stars in the sky," he said.

"Aha, you've been busy!"

"Yes, and I started at a very old age, so don't be worried, Talia. Let me tell you my view in relation to your question. Love between men and women should be based on respect. Respect for yourself, first of all. Then you can respect your partner. When you choose the right partner, you have to choose someone who is similar to your own nature. Then you will be able to understand that whatever develops from your relationship is blessed. The other person helps you to become who you are by reacting to you. Sometimes it's difficult, but he is like a mirror to you. He gives you responses to your own behaviour, he gives you the chance to be who you are and also to change your own behaviour out of respect.

You must choose to look for the positive in him all the time, because it is very easy to stay focused on the negatives, especially when someone is very close to you. That is the secret of a good relationship. Understand that this is a gift because it helps you to become who you are. The key is to find the right man. The 'clear mirror' for you. Talia, I want you to ask Bob about this because his relationship with Miya was always so secret."

"You already said it so well. What else can I add?" said Bob.

"Come on, Bob," Said Dror. *"There is a rumour that you are a virgin."* All the men started to laugh.

"Okay, I will clear this up," said Bob. *"I agree with Dror one hundred percent. The only time you swear in the name of God is when you get married. And why is that? It's because you actually say to God that you can take this challenge to help you to approach more closely to Him. You agree to deal with whatever comes through it, to help you become a better person. If you deal just with yourself, you can easily think you are perfect, and you won't be challenged. Nobody will complain about your behaviour. Believe me - and the billions of other people around the world that sometimes get really annoyed when someone complains. But you have to understand: you never know what will help you become who you should be. Without a motivating stimulus, you will not develop. Sometimes it can be annoying, but it will help you to realise your full potential. Because of this, I always recommend that people do not compare their relationships to others. That is*

why I never spoke about my relationship with Miya. It is just between me, her, and of course, God."

Mustafa started to laugh loudly. *"Again, you didn't tell us anything! Okay, okay, Talia. I will tell you my view. First of all, I agree with all my dear friends here. I just want to relax you here because I feel your question comes from your stress about your age. My first wife was forty years old when I married her, and we had six children. Don't be stressed, my lovely Talia, about your age. You remember we talked about focusing on the positives? When you are with someone that is right for you, you will learn not to be selfish because you always need to consider the other person. The kinder you become to your partner, the more you accept each other, the better you will become. First of all, the key is to find the man who is right for you. If you are with someone who is not willing to make the same effort as you, you actually don't have a partner to work with."*

"Beautiful," said Lori. *"I agree with all of you, my dearest friends. Let me show you another way to look at this. Not everyone has to get married or have a partner. At the end of the day, you come alone to this world, and you die alone. If you don't find the right man, Talia, you will most certainly get challenged by other people in this life. You can't jump into the pool and stay dry. People are the mirror that helps you look inside yourself, whether they are your partner or your friends. They are the gift and the chance to become who you can be."*

"Wow, thank you so much," I said. *"That's beautiful."*

"Hey," said Bob. *"I got a message from the Joker!"*

"What? Who is the Joker?" I asked.

"Ah," said Dror. *"Everyone knows who the Joker is."*

"But not everyone accepts him," said Lori.

"Aha," said Mustafa. *"He is the reason for all reasons."*

"He has infinite names," said Dror. *"Everyone calls him by different names. But all of us, when we are together, we call him the Joker."*

Bob said, *"If people twist the truth about what we have said, they have made up even more stories about the Joker. Listen to this, Talia. They say that the Joker is against sex and against people who are gay. They say that the Joker punishes people."*

"Yes, yes," said Mustafa. *"They also say that he doesn't care about people who suffer. That he doesn't do anything to help poor, miserable people."*

"Yes," said Lori. *"I also hear that they blame him all the time for creating disasters, as if he tests people."*

Dror said, *"He actually doesn't want anything. He doesn't have need. All he did was bring his own children to the backyard to play."*

"So what did he say?" Dror asked Bob.

"He said we need to go to Jerusalem to teach the people there how to play Union. One moment, Talia, don't go. Let me take a photo of you to send to the Joker. When I say two, smile. One, two."

"Aha," said Bob. "You got a like from the Joker. And a message. Listen to this! The Joker said 'nice tits.'"

"What?!" I said.

"Yes," said Bob. "He said you need to show off your balcony more."

"What does that mean? That's not a nice thing to say to me!"

"Oh, Talia," said Dror. "That is so typical. You get a nice compliment, and you complain about it. Saying, 'What does it mean? What does it mean?'"

"Aha," said Lori. "It's a good message from the Joker. You know what message other people get?"

"No, but it's not funny," I said.

"Hey, Talia," said Bob. "You lost your sense of humour!"

"One second," said Lori. "Where is Talia's sense of humour? Let's look for it."

"Hey, maybe it's on the table," said Bob.

"No, on the chair," said Dror. "No, no, I found it on the floor."

I stood up from my chair. Mustafa came close to me and held both of my hands. *"Hey, Talia, don't be upset. It's a good message from the Joker. The Joker always talks with symbols. He wants you to figure out what this means. He wants the power to be in your hands. It's like, if I was to give you a treasure, you wouldn't appreciate it as much as if you had personally had to dig in the ground for a few days and then found it for yourself. 'Beautiful tits' means... means beautiful heart, and 'show your balcony,' Talia, means that you need to speak your own truth."*

Speak your own truth . . . speak your own truth . . . speak your own truth . . . speak your own truth . . .

I heard these words echoing from far away. My alarm woke me up from a deep sleep. It was 5.00 am in Bangkok. That was a dream.

Yes, I will speak my own truth.

<u>*Top Meeting Real Characters:*</u>
Dror Abraham
Rob Jesus
Mustafa Mohamed
Lori Boudahha
Joker
God

DEATH

My darling, my love, my only one. In my life, I have never had a near- death experience or anything close to that. I know people who have had such experiences without drugs, but nobody in the whole world can convince me differently than this, that the highest and greatest illusion in this *'world of illusion'* is death. Death does not exist.

It's hard to understand, but it's true: your body dies, but not your soul. Not who you really are. It's like now, my darling, I'm here in the world of illusion, writing to you, while you are on the other side. I can feel you. I'm close to you. Just the element of this world separates us. One day you will be here in the world of illusion, and I will be in the other side. What then? Nothing. I will always be with you, loving you as I am now. It's hard to be separate from someone close. The element of the world of illusion starts to work. We can't reach the person who passed away. The process of grief is important. But, more important, is letting go, because while we hold on to them, the person who has passed away can see and feel our grief. They also experience happiness, they feel as free as a bird, and they want to say to us, "Hey, I feel good! I feel love!" But they can't. It's even more difficult for them than it is for us who stay here in this world.

When we go to the theatre and the show finishes, the curtain closes. Where did everyone go? The guests and the players, everyone goes to their own home. When we finish our life here and close the curtain of our eyes, we also go to our home. There is one destination that all of us want to reach, which is the big magnet: Pure Love. But to be able to reach it, you need to be at the right station. To be able to hear the music on the radio, you need to find the right radio channel. The sperm that can connect with the ovary is the strongest one. You have to be ready. This is the chance that life gives us.

Death is a gift from the universe, just as life is. Life gives us experience to remind us who we are, really. Life gives us again and again the chance to choose and to be guided by our soul. All our difficulty is a gift because when we choose the right way to deal with it, we are no longer guided by our weakness. We become more soulful.

It's like when you are driving, and the traffic lights change to yellow, but you have time to slow down, maybe even to stop. If you do that, maybe you can look around and see something unexpected and beautiful, or something that may remind you of something important that you may need to do. Or you can choose to ignore the yellow light and speed through very fast before it turns red. In this instance, you can miss the beauty and the potential reminder.

When you deal with difficulty and challenges, you can slow down. Maybe stop and ask, *'What is life trying to show me here?'*, *'What do I need to figure out?'* *'What challenge do I have here?'* *'What do I need to overcome here?'*, *'What gift can I get here?'* And more importantly, *'What is the right way for me to choose to deal with this difficulty that will help me to grow?'* All the people you will meet, my love. All the places you will visit, my love. All the difficulty you will deal with, my love. All the love you will receive, my love, for good and for bad. They want for you just one thing: they want you to be you, to be back to yourself. To be as big as you can, and as powerful as you can. To be an *'Explosion of Love!'*

They will help you, they will help you, they will be nasty to you, they will be horrible to you, they will touch you, they hurt you, they spoil you, they hug you, they test you, they will dishonor you, but most importantly, they will all guide you back to yourself.

All of us have limited time on Earth. Everyone has a different story. When our time comes to the end, we undress our physical body, we undress our feelings and thoughts, and fly to the other realm with only our soul and our memories and experiences. This is when we die from this world and are born again in the next realm.

Another way of thinking about this is that when we are born, we dress in a physical body, we wear feelings and thoughts, but we always have our soul in life and in death. That always exists. We always take our soul with us, in whatever realm we travel to. That's who we are – pure soul – and because of that, death is not the end, it's just a transition. Life is part of this if our soul chooses to be here, my darling, my love. If your soul chooses to be here, if you decide that this realm can help you in your journey, then hurry and join me. You're choosing me as your mum, it is my honour, my dream, my wish to be chosen by you.

And now, darling, our story is coming to the end. From being born to our death. And from the other realm – wherever you are now – to be born here. I have tried from the depths of my heart to tell you a story about life, about the bright life from my experience. How to choose to be fully alive in life.

I hope you don't feel stressed or pushed by me to come here. That is not my intention. I want you to know that if you come here, I promise I will be as honest and real as I can. It doesn't matter what I'm telling you here, or which story this is. It matters how you will see me in your eyes. How I will be with you. How I will react to you. What it will be. My attitude to you, to my family, to your father and his family. To the people around me. How I treat my life, myself. My attitude for myself, for others. What is my attitude for money, how I spend my time? We learn from people's actions, not by their words. Only if you choose to come here, if you're not, that's not a problem. I understand. After all, I ask for you something big: I ask for you to be born and wear a body, and come to the illusion world. And for me.

Not everyone needs the experience of parenthood by loving and taking care of someone for all their life. But I do believe God gives us this present of motherhood because He wants us to be like Him – to lend our hearts to someone else, to love unconditionally. But not everyone needs this experience, and I know – my darling – our love and connection are above this existence. It's above and infinite. It's in our soul. If you decide to not come here (and your dick-head Dad doesn't arrive here soon), I will wait patiently to the end of my life, and then I will fly to you straight away.

My love, my darling. Do not come here for me, but rather come here for yourself.

Well, how can I say that? How can I express my feelings in this manner? The ability to express our feelings in a True language is limited by vocabulary. It doesn't exist in any of the world's languages, whether they are modern or ancient languages, including the language of nature, the language of animals, and the language of the angels. It hasn't been written in songs, scripts, or books; it hasn't played at the cinema or on the stage; it hasn't been seen yet. Romeo and Juliet never even got close to expressing love, as much as I love you. I'm here waiting for you.

Until the moment that you come, and we meet in this world of illusion, it's always:

You. Me. Love. God. Amen.

H a l l e l u j a h.